Black and Presbyterian

Black and Presbyterian

The Heritage and the Hope

Revised and Enlarged

Gayraud S. Wilmore

Witherspoon Press
Louisville, Kentucky

Scripture quotations in this publication are from the New Revised Standard
Version of the Bible, copyright © 1989 by the Division of Christian Education of
the National Council of the Churches of Christ in the U.S.A. Used by permission.

Every effort has been made to trace copyrights on the materials included in
this book. If any copyrighted material has nevertheless been included without
permission and due acknowledgment, proper credit will be inserted in future
printings after notice has been received.

Edited by Beth Basham
Cover and interior design by Pip Pullen

Published by Witherspoon Press, a Ministry of the General Assembly Council,
Presbyterian Church (U.S.A.), Louisville, Kentucky

www.pcusa.org/witherspoonpress

PRINTED IN THE UNITED STATES OF AMERICA

07 08 09 — 10 9 8 7 6 5 4 3 2

Library of Congress Cataloging-in-Publication Data

Wilmore, Gayraud S., date.
    Black and Presbyterian : the heritage and the hope /
Gayraud S. Wilmore—Rev. and enl.
        p.   cm.
    Includes bibliographical references.
    ISBN 1-57895-049-X
        1. Afro-American Presbyterians.   I. Title.
BX8946.A35W54 1998
285'.1'08996073—dc21   97-48974

Contents

Preface to the Revised Edition

Black and Presbyterian: The Heritage and the Hope, first published by Geneva Press in 1983, has been out of print for several years. The demand for a revised edition has been growing as African Americans continue to remain in and join the Presbyterian Church (U.S.A.). The 1983 reunion of the northern and southern branches of the church created many problems for Black Presbyterians—not the least being the further dilution of our numerical strength at every level when another million Whites were added, many of whom had limited, if any, understanding and appreciation of the Black presence within Presbyterianism. Black Presbyterians, North and South, are still asking the questions about cultural differences, identity, and ethnic-specific mission that they asked before the reunion—asking these questions with even more urgency in a church and nation where racism seems unabated. Is it possible or more difficult than in 1980 to experience what Black Presbyterians United (BPU) President Claude C. Kilgore called "unity within diversity"?

The Southeast Region of the National Black Presbyterian Caucus (NBPC), successor to BPU, held its annual meeting in 1994 in Atlanta, where Professor Wilmore has made his home since retiring from the faculty of the Interdenominational Theological Center in 1990. At that meeting, held in the New Life Presbyterian Church, Professor Wilmore talked about the need to fill the hole created by the continued absence of a popular history of Black Presbyterians, our problems, restlessness, heritage, and hope for whatever future God wills for African American children in this church.

It was in Atlanta in 1994 that we began to talk about the possibility of a revision of Black and Presbyterian. At first Professor Wilmore thought he would update the story of Inez Jones and her husband, the mythical couple whose experience in the church paralleled that of so many of us who have struggled against racial and cultural insensitivity in the church. This story is not included in the revised edition, however, because of the need to face head-on some new and larger issues; for example, whether or not African Americans should remain in the reunited denomination or form a new church that would more fairly represent our cultural and theological distinctions.

As I listened to Professor Wilmore visualize his perspective for the end of the century, I found myself becoming enthusiastic about bringing the Black Presbyterian story up to date. At that meeting I pledged to present the idea of a revised edition of Black and Presbyterian to the NBPC Board of Directors and see the project through to a successful completion.

The Board, which now owns the rights to this book and will continue (as with the first edition) to plow the royalties back into the caucus, accepted the challenge, and Dr. Wilmore agreed to do a thorough revision of the original text. What follows, therefore, is a monograph, close to the original, but casting some new light on the history, problems, hopes, and aspirations of African American Presbyterians on the brink of the twenty-first century. It will focus on the thoughts and energies we will need in the new millennium. It does not pretend to be a comprehensive treatment of the history of Blacks in American Presbyterianism. That work, begun by the late Professor Andrew E. Murray of Lincoln University, Pennsylvania, in his *Presbyterians and the Negro—A History* (Philadelphia: Presbyterian Historical Society, 1966), still needs to be written, and we eagerly wait for some enterprising Black scholar to undertake the difficult job that the research and writing of such a comprehensive history will require.

In the meantime, Dr. Wilmore has provided us with an abbreviated, easy-to-read, lay-oriented interpretation of the story of Black Presbyterians that can be used for individual and group study. The Board of Directors of the NBPC would like to express its thanks to him and to Donna Blackstock, associate director of the Curriculum Publishing Program Area of the Presbyterian Church (U.S.A.), for making it possible for all of us to revisit this heritage and this hope—with all its warts, blemishes, pains, pleasures, failures, and victories.

I also agreed to approach some of our largest African American Presbyterian congregations for aid to defray the costs of this project. On behalf of the NBPC Board, I offer sincere thanks to the following pastors and churches who contributed to the funding that helped to make this revised edition possible: Rev. Dr. William G. Gillespie, Pastor of Cote Brilliante Presbyterian Church, St. Louis, Missouri; Rev. John F. Warner, Pastor of Crerar Memorial Presbyterian Church, Chicago, Illinois; Rev. Robert Burkins, Pastor of Elmwood Presbyterian Church, East Orange, New Jersey; Rev. Dr. Lonnie Oliver, Pastor of New Life Presbyterian Church, Atlanta, Georgia; Rev. Leon E. Fanniel, Pastor of St. Paul United Presbyterian Church, Los Angeles, California; Rev. Dr. Charles Marks, Pastor of Witherspoon Presbyterian Church, Indianapolis, Indiana; and Rev. Dr. Joe W. Rigsby, Pastor of Woodlawn Presbyterian Church, Jacksonville, Florida.

It is with overflowing gratitude, esteem, and a profound awareness of the many blessings that their lives and ministries gave and continue to give to the caucus and to the whole Presbyterian Church that we dedicate this book to the memory of Rev. Clarence S. Cave, Rev. Dr. H. Eugene Farlough, Jr., Rev. Kermit Overton, and Elder George McDonald. May they smile upon us, knowing that we are trying to carry on the work that they cared about so much.

Jesse C. Swanigan, Former President
National Black Presbyterian Caucus
University City, Missouri

Preface to the First Edition

The idea for this book came out of a lively conversation between the author and a group of ministers and seminary students in California. In May 1980, Gayraud S. Wilmore was the commencement speaker at San Francisco Theological Seminary in San Anselmo. Taking advantage of his presence on the West Coast, a group of Black clergy and seminarians and I arranged to have him remain for a few days to lead us in some reflection and discussion about Black Presbyterians: Who are we? Where did we come from? What did we hope for in this church? At the end of the conference we talked about a book on the subject. Professor Wilmore roughed out an outline on the plane back to Rochester, New York. After it had been circulated among some West Coast leaders of Black Presbyterians United (BPU), we agreed that the book should be written and made available to the entire Presbyterian family as soon as possible.

What follows in these pages is essentially an expansion of the lectures given at San Anselmo. Professor Wilmore lays out in clear and concise language the meaning of the Black religious experience, but particularly the pain and agony, the joys and exhilarations of being a Black Presbyterian. His treatment of the history of Blacks in the Presbyterian Church is brief but refreshing and informative. The enigmas and contradictions related to our presence within this predominantly White church are candidly faced. Professor Wilmore explores the reasons why Black believers, despite all the problems, would not be denied the opportunity to witness to Jesus Christ as Savior and Liberator through the instrumentality of a predominantly White and often racist institution.

This book has relevance for the discussion now going on in several denominations about the role and status of Black members. Lay people and clergy within the United Church of Christ, the United Methodist Church, the Disciples of Christ, the Episcopal Church, the American Baptist Churches, and several other denominations will find that the issues raised here are all too familiar. White Christians in these denominations, as well as within Presbyterianism, will learn how better to relate to their Black brothers and sisters, and to the brothers and sisters of other ethnic groups, by reading and discussing this book.

A variety of purposes are served by the publication of this book at this time. It will contribute to the celebration of the 175th anniversary of Black Presbyterianism in the United States by reminding us of the rich history of our involvement in the denomination; it will provide a study and discussion resource for the laity around the meaning of Black culture, the theological insights that arise from our journey, and the identity crisis that Black middle-class Christians are facing in this post–civil rights period; it will make some valuable suggestions about how Black Christians generally, and Black Presbyterians particularly, ought to be relating to the Black communities around the country of which they are a part.

This book, in short, should help Black Presbyterians get in touch with themselves as they reflect upon their history and the mission they should be about today. Others who read these pages will learn of the sacrifices and gifts of Blacks to the life and development of Presbyterianism in the United States at a time when the reunion of its two largest branches is anticipated. All Presbyterians need to appreciate what the Afro-American constituency has contributed to and what it demands from the newly reunited church.

This book was commissioned by Black Presbyterians United. Its publication was made possible, in part, by a generous gift from one of its friends of long standing. Black Presbyterians United, the national Black caucus of the denomination, extends its heartfelt thanks to Gayraud S. Wilmore for presenting to the Presbyterian family—lay and clergy, at home and abroad—a challenging study worthy of consideration by every member of the denomination as we all strive for the "unity within diversity" that God wills for the whole church of Christ.

Claude C. Kilgore, National President
Black Presbyterians United
Los Angeles, California

So it makes little sense to insist that there is no such thing as a Black or an African American Christianity.

1   What Is African American Christianity?

Before the reader turns another page, we need to address the problem of terminology. When words such as *African American, Euro-American, White,* and *Black* are used to modify nouns such as *religion* or *Christianity,* many folks are quickly turned off. Most of us like to believe that because we live in the modern world, where everyone wants first to be recognized as a human being who is created in the image of God, there is no reason to classify each other in ways that draw attention to our differences. Why is it necessary, many will ask, to throw up artificial barriers between us by insisting on a Black or African American Christianity instead of just plain Christianity, or Black or White Presbyterians instead of just plain Presbyterians? One might have used these terms in the 1960s and made sense, but why should anyone read this book on the brink of the second millennium of the Christian era?

Some will have an even more basic objection. "What," they will ask, "does the Bible have to say about a *Black* Christianity or a *White* Christianity? Show me those terms in my family Bible, Preacher! Then maybe we'll have something to discuss. Otherwise, just talk to me about Christianity, pure and simple, and leave out all that racial and ethnic stuff."

Of course, such a request is not unreasonable; it just happens to be pointless if we're really interested in examining the state of the Christian faith in the world we read about every day in the newspaper. If there ever was anything about Christianity that was "pure and simple," it evaporated sometime before the end of the first century A.D. The way Christianity has come down to us today makes it a very mixed bag of racial/ethnic, or cultural and religious, traditions and understandings that may or may not—depending how they are transmitted and by whom—help someone to know who Jesus Christ is and what he wants his modern-day disciples to believe and do.

Nor is it possible to run to the Bible every time we try to escape this problem. We cannot even hear or tell a simple biblical story about the birth of Jesus, his first sermon in his hometown of Nazareth, or his parable about the man who was robbed on the Jericho road without consciously and unconsciously filtering it through the sieve of our different languages, the time and place of our rearing, our age and gender cohort, our racial, ethnic, and cultural locations in the biosphere, the level of our education, our psychosomatic condition, our economic and social status, our political convictions, and so forth.

The Bible does not speak to us as if we were purely disembodied spirits floating around in some celestial vacuum, but in the only way human beings can hear God's voice and recognize it as truth for themselves. The Bible speaks to us in a way that takes into account all the dirt and grime of our personal and social existence, who we really are in the bathroom as well as the sanctuary, our given time and place in history. If we insist, therefore, that the Scriptures must be the exclusive judge of how the term *Christianity* should or should not be modified, we should at least be aware that the word *Christian* appears only three times in the Bible (Acts 11:26; 26:28; and 1 Peter 4:16), and the word *Christianity* does not appear! We use both these terms to describe the peculiar religion that formed itself, albeit by the power of the Holy Spirit, around the personality and ministry of Jesus long after both he and those who knew him in the flesh had passed off this earthly scene.

So where does all that leave us?

It leaves us with the difficulty that when we use the term *Christianity* we are speaking, whether we intend to or not, as if we were primarily concerned with history, with systems of beliefs, practices, and social structures that have grown up around the memory and teachings of the man called Jesus. Take it or leave it.

Someone will retort, more or less angrily: "Hold on there, Preacher! You're not talking about *me*. I have absolutely no concern about such things. I'm only interested in the pure and unadulterated gospel!"

Well, it's hard to know how to satisfy such a "pure and unadulterated" interest. Because the gospel, that is, the good news about Jesus, comes packaged in the wrappings of so many different kinds of languages, cultures, and ways of looking at reality—some ancient, some modern, and some postmodern—not even its essential message can be extracted without an interpretive posture (something biblical scholars call *hermeneutics*) that comes preliminary to comprehension and involves much more than reading a series of words on a printed page.

Both in ordinary conversation and in technical writing we use the word *Christianity* to connote the particular system of beliefs, ritual practices, and sociological characteristics of the religion about Jesus as understood in various contexts. When we speak of Early Christianity we imply that system in its first two or three centuries; when we speak of Western Christianity we mean that system as it developed with Rome as its center instead of Constantinople; when we speak of Black Christianity we refer to that system as it predominates in African and African American communities rather than in European or Euro-American (we'll sometimes use the term *North Atlantic*) communities.

Thus, in the first instance we focus on the religion from the perspective of time; in the second, from the perspective of geographical or geopolitical factors; and in the third, from the perspective of race ethnicity or culture.

In none of these contexts can we pretend that the Bible is the primary and exclusive source of the information we seek. We may, of course, consult Scripture about the particular features of the church in, say, the late first century A.D. But what we learn in the text will tell us very little about Christianity in the Middle Ages, in Puritan New England, or among Negroes in the United States at the beginning of the Civil War. Let us not ask the Bible to do what it was never intended to do.

A Social and Cultural Fact of Life

So it makes little sense to insist that there is no such thing as a Black or an African American Christianity. Even if you want to argue that we're talking about Jesus Christ and not about Christianity, and that Jesus Christ is "the same yesterday and today and forever," as the writer of Heb. 13:8 tells us, we must concede that the way the religion (or faith, if you prefer) about him developed in different times, in various parts of the world, and among diverse peoples is a cultural and societal fact that reasonable people have to take seriously.

We may *profess* that we are interested only in some unadulterated form of the faith that takes no account of these things, but upon an honest investigation we would find it practically impossible to describe that form without certain social and cultural accretions sticking to our description.

We may as well be honest about it. Both the sins and the virtues of humankind are all too obvious in any study of Christianity. There is really no point in being so coy about why and how it developed among African Americans as to reject out of hand the idea of a Black or African American Christianity among other forms of the faith. Is there any reason to doubt that the Holy Spirit, given to lead us into the truth, has been able to use our form as well as other forms? The apostle Paul confessed, "I have become all things to all people, that I might by all means save some" (1 Cor. 9:22).

To speak or write about an African American Christianity is to refer to a social and cultural reality for more than four hundred years in what used to be called the New World; that during most of those years—like it or not—85 to 90 percent of all Black Christians have worshiped with their own race in all-Black conventicles or congregations. Certain characteristics of faith and life, belief and behavior, have resulted from that simple (we probably should say complex) fact. To acknowledge those characteristics and study them is to neither condemn nor commend them. Indeed, we will have occasion in this book to say something on both sides of that divide. But at the moment we want only to establish the reasonableness, even the correctness, of the terminology we will be using in this book.

The Christianization of Africans in America

In this small study we cannot hope to survey the whole history of Christianity among African Americans in the United States, much less among African Americans in Canada, the Caribbean, and Central and South America. And unfortunately, we have to leave out altogether what Christianity looked like in Africa, particularly in Egypt, Ethiopia, and Nubia, almost a thousand years before Europeans began in earnest to explore the west and east coasts of the continent of our ancestors. Even apart from these important considerations, we would have more than could be contained in a much larger work if we were to discuss Black religion that has existed in all parts of our Western Hemisphere for hundreds of years—sometimes as Christianity, sometimes in forms assumed to be antagonistic to Christianity, sometimes as a mixture of Christianity and some other religion—notably as neo-African cults and sects. All of that is a part of the whole story, but the whole story will have to be left for another book.

Slavery and Christianity

At first the English settlers of the North American colonies did not intend to make their slaves Christians. That was considered a dangerous practice, for a baptized slave might get the foolish idea that freedom in Christ (Gal. 5:1) had to include freedom from bondage. The conversion of slaves was also thought to be unreasonable, because who would suppose that people who were believed to be little more than savages could understand the Christian religion well enough to be benefitted by it?

There were, however, always a few White people who insisted on trying to convert African slaves. The bishops of London, prelates of the Anglican Church, felt some responsibility and instructed priests of the Church of England in the colonies to minister to Black slaves. The Society of Friends, or Quakers, tried to give them religious instruction. Beginning with Rev. Samuel Davies in Virginia, even the Presbyterians showed some interest. By 1757 Davies reported that he had baptized at least 150 Negroes, after preaching to them for about eighteen months.

The major credit for getting a revival started among the slaves in the South must go to the Separatist Baptists. They were rough-hewn, evangelistically minded frontier preachers, many of whom came from New England, who built many churches in the plantation country of the Carolinas and Georgia. There was also a group called "Methodist societies" that broke away from the Church of England after the Revolutionary War and encouraged the slaves to join them and even preach to White people. These two denominations, the Baptists and the Methodists, made the most consistent and enthusiastic effort to Christianize the Africans in North America. After 1750 they were attracting increasing numbers of slaves to their services—mostly to the displeasure of many slaveholders who correctly suspected that only mischief could come out of this kind of imprudent evangelism.

Scholars are now fairly confident that the first slaves to become Christians, and many who came after them, held on to certain features of the religions they or their parents had practiced in Africa. In Africa they had recognized a Supreme or High God. That concept was not new to them. They also had practiced assembling for prayer, ritual worship, and a form of water baptism, so some aspects of Christian belief and practice were not difficult for them to accept.

Where they adopted new ideas and rituals that were similar to the old ones they knew back home, the African forms were strengthened rather than discarded, although it is more accurate to say that they were gradually transformed. The Africanized Christianity that flourished on southern plantations, often to the disgust and dismay of the White missionaries, included some characteristics that were unfamiliar to White Christians. For example, there was much dancing and singing in the African style of "call and response"; drumming (whenever permitted, for the masters were afraid that drums might signal revolt); elaborate nighttime funeral customs; spirit possession (or what we later called "getting happy"); and conversion experiences that involved flying, traveling great distances, or encountering spirit guides, of one kind or another, in dreams and visions.

Bishop Daniel A. Payne of the African Methodist Episcopal Church found the "ring shout,"[1] an unmistakable retention from the African past, being practiced in urban African Methodist Episcopal (AME) congregations well into the late nineteenth century.* It is now almost the twenty-first century, but we wouldn't have to search very hard in most American cities to find something very close to the ring shout today.

Black Christianity continued to retain African features, particularly where the Whites granted Black preachers the freedom to organize "independent" Black congregations. The African Baptist or Bluestone Baptist Church appeared in 1758 near to present-day Mecklenburg, Virginia; and in 1773 slave preachers David George and George Lisle had a slave congregation at Silver Bluff, South Carolina, just across the Savannah River from Augusta, Georgia. There was a flourishing congregation in Williamsburg, Virginia, as early as 1776. We can assume that these were all Christian churches that had a decided African twist!

In the North, Black Methodist and Episcopal churches were founded in Philadelphia by Richard Allen and Absalom Jones before 1794. A group of African Methodists had split from the White St. George's Methodist Church

---

*The author and publisher have made every attempt to document and research the quoted material included in this revised edition. Since the publication of the first edition, most of the author's research, which was conducted at the Presbyterian Historical Society in Philadelphia and the Schomburg Center in New York City, is now inaccessible. "When I wrote the book in 1980," says Wilmore, "I was probably influenced by the success of Nathan T. Huggins's *Black Odyssey: The African American Ordeal in Slavery* (New York: Random House, 1978), which has no notes. . . . The style is conversational and storytelling, rather than a work of 'scientific historiography.'"

in Philadelphia seven years before and were quickly followed by Black members of White congregations in Baltimore, New York City, Wilmington, Charleston, and elsewhere. A fever for independent churches, under the leadership of Black pastors, was abroad in the free African American communities of the North. Such freedom was, of course, violently repressed in the South for many years before the Civil War, although a few independent churches flourished under White surveillance. But in the North most African American converts increasingly became members of churches led by preachers of their own color. In the South, where the slaves continued to worship with their masters in segregated pews, many nonordained Black preachers carried on an "invisible institution" behind the backs of the slaveowners and were ready to claim their people as soon as emancipation came.

A Church of the Oppressed

The African American church from the beginning was obsessed with the idea of freedom from slavery. That is probably the most important thing that can be said about it. The AMEs began with a revolt against White religious control that could not obscure their dissatisfaction with their civil condition as well. In the Deep South, three of the four earliest Black Baptist preachers that we know about—David George, George Lisle, and Amos Williams—fled slavery and founded new congregations in Nova Scotia, Jamaica, and the Bahamas. That's why we must insist that in its basic theology, as well as its liturgical style, African American Christianity was a religion of freedom; the church was the center of a partly religious, partly secular movement whose intention was to bring about the total abolition of slavery.

After the Civil War and during the Reconstruction Era, the churches were at the forefront of the attempt to complete the work of emancipation from which the North was swiftly retreating. Many African American preachers went into politics in the repressed states of the former Confederacy and were involved in the so-called Freedmen's agencies that were initially created to help Congress administer the Reconstruction. The three great concerns of our churches during the remainder of the nineteenth century were missions to the recently freed people, education—particularly the kind introduced by Booker T. Washington at Tuskegee Institute in Alabama—and, surprisingly, African missions, including selective immigration to Africa that was promoted by such clergy as the AME Bishop Henry McNeal Turner and Edward Wilmot Blyden, a Black Presbyterian minister and educator born in the Virgin Islands.

In no other period did the masses of African Americans in the United States need the church more desperately than between the turn of the century and the Great Depression of the 1930s. Whatever civil rights African Americans enjoyed immediately following the Civil War had eroded by 1914, on the eve of the First World War. Indeed, Blacks were more segregated and discriminated against during and after the war than they were in 1850. The South struck back with a vengeance, and the North supinely imitated its former enemies. Racism became rife in all parts of the nation. In the South and border states, the Ku Klux Klan and other anti-Negro hate groups were involved in a wave of lynchings and race riots. In the North, almost three million impoverished agricultural workers and tenant farmers from rural Dixie had their hopes for a better life crushed in the overcrowded urban ghettos of the industrial cities between 1890 and 1929. They were part of one of the greatest mass migrations in the history of the Western world, but it was a migration from one oppression to another.

During the Great Depression, Black city churches were under severe pressure. They braced themselves to receive the migrants but were finally overwhelmed by the need of social services for people who often arrived in Baltimore, Chicago, or Detroit with all their earthly possessions in a burlap sack. Moreover, they found themselves losing out in competition with new sects and cults that sprang up in the slums to feed the psychological and sometimes physical hungers that our mainline denominations seemed powerless to satisfy. In the case of quasi-secular movements such as Father Divine's Peace Mission, Bishop "Daddy" Grace's House of Prayer for All People, the Moorish Science Temples, and the Universal Negro Improvement Association of Marcus Garvey, some of the economic and political, as well as social and spiritual, needs of the newcomers were met. And riding high on the crest of the concentric waves of Black Pentecostalism that poured out of Los Angeles in 1905 were both jazzy storefront churches and the hard-eyed cultic movements whose charismatic leaders attracted more of the people at the bottom of the heap than were drawn to what Carter G. Woodson calls the socially conscious "institutional churches."

Whether storefront or renovated Gothic cathedral, the church of the masses was a church of an oppressed race. In every city a few mainstream congregations tried to meet the needs of the migrants and projected an image of racial pride and self-help. Those churches became an important base for politics when organizations like the National Association for the Advancement of Colored

People gradually took over the leadership of the masses. But between the two world wars, African American Methodists, Baptists, Congregationalists, Presbyterians, and Episcopalians were to see a steady diminution of their influence. Although their power over the people was never totally destroyed, mainstream religious institutions in the North all but collapsed before the unremitting onslaught of anticlericalism, secularism, and nihilism in the African American urban communities during the first half of the twentieth century.

By the end of the Second World War many observers had pronounced the Negro church less than useful in the climb of its people out of poverty and second-class citizenship. That judgment is probably too harsh, but there is no question that the middle-class African American churches fell on difficult times. Black clergy, almost 90 percent without formal theological education, were said to be good for only two things: preaching hellfire damnation and raising money. The highly esteemed Black sociologist E. Franklin Frazier wrote that the church of the masses, more than any other institution, was responsible for the "backwardness" of the race.

The Era of Dr. Martin Luther King Jr.

At this lowest point of their influence, the African American churches were suddenly jolted into a new maturity when an AME laywoman, Mrs. Rosa Parks, refused to sit in the segregated section of a city bus in Montgomery, Alabama. The year was 1955. A young Baptist minister from Atlanta named Martin Luther King Jr. took up her cause by mobilizing Blacks to stay off the buses. The Montgomery Bus Boycott demonstrated that despite the decline of church authority, when organized and inspired by their traditional religious leaders, African Americans were capable of exercising extraordinary economic and political power. The movement caught on like wildfire, and at one point in the early 1960s the Southern Regional Council reported sixty or more local organizations in various towns across the nation, led by clergy and carrying on nonviolent direct action in affiliation with King's Southern Christian Leadership Conference (SCLC).

Out of this new mass movement, the first one since Garveyism, came the widespread civil disorders of the North in the mid-1960s and the Black Power movement of 1965. Although many northern churches were implicated in what happened, Dr. King and other mainstream leaders dissociated themselves from the call for Black Power. But there were other ministers and lay people—

particularly in the hardened cities of the North and West—who supported the young revolutionaries and Black self-determination without condoning the anarchy in the slogan "Burn, Baby, Burn!" On the heels of the northern city rebellions of 1964–1967, the National Conference of Black Churchmen (NCBC), a group of Black Power–oriented religious leaders, moved many African American church people from a moderate social gospel Christianity toward a new Black theology, political radicalism, and Pan-Africanism. Dr. King, perhaps without realizing it, had created a new African American consciousness in the churches that was to continue for the rest of the century.

It was in connection with this new Black consciousness that the African American caucuses of the predominantly White denominations joined the struggle. Among them was a group called Concerned Presbyterians, later, Black Presbyterians United, and presently, the National Black Presbyterian Caucus. We will soon take a closer look at these groups, but first we will interrupt this synopsis of African American church history to examine the meaning of the distinctive religious impulses that emanate from African American Christianity. Perhaps then we can better understand what it is. What *kind* of Christianity was evolving in the slave community during all those bitter years prior to Emancipation, and what did it look like after the mass migrations that brought the dark children of Africa out of the South and scattered them across the broad lap of the nation?

Questions for Discussion

Scripture for Reflection: James 1:27

1. At the beginning of this chapter it is suggested that many will ask the following question: "Why is it necessary to speak of an African American Christianity instead of just plain Christianity?"

   ◆ Do you agree that our understanding of any biblical text is affected by language, age, gender, race, education, and environment?

   ◆ If you tend to agree, list three examples that support your point of view.

   ◆ If you tend to disagree, list three examples to support your convictions.

2. Why do you think the eleven o'clock hour on Sunday mornings is the most segregated hour of the week?

3. Consider carefully the following statement: The conversion of slaves was also thought to be unreasonable, because who would suppose that people who were believed to be little more than savages could understand the Christian religion well enough to be benefited by it? How does this statement impact your views on African American Christianity?

4. Discuss how the purposes or goals of African American Christians might differ from the purposes or goals of European Christians.

5. Cite the three great concerns of African American churches in the nineteenth century. What should the concerns of the African American church be for the twenty-first century?

6. Is it more important to strive toward a unified church, the Presbyterian Church (U.S.A.), than to invest our time and energy in finding a separate identity at this juncture in our history? Can't we all just get along?

But remember that what we are suggesting is merely a useful model for examining the complex makeup of African American religion, not the bed of the legendary Procrustes, who stretched or cut off the legs of his victims to make them fit!

Major Strands of a Complex Tradition

rom the beginning of the Atlantic slave trade to the first decades of the twentieth century, three characteristic orientations, or subtraditions, developed in the religion of the African American people. Although we can identify all three where slaves and free Blacks lived and worshiped in the same geographical area, changing historical conditions generally forced these subtraditions, or tendencies, to appear in a rough developmental sequence. We may call the oldest the survival tradition, a later one the liberation tradition, and the third and most recent one the elevation tradition. But remember that what we are suggesting is merely a useful model for examining the complex makeup of African American religion, not the bed of the legendary Procrustes, who stretched or cut off the legs of his victims to make them fit! We must not forget that in the late nineteenth century, and more often in our own time, these subtraditions may seem to operate simultaneously in various and complex ways in the same churches and communities.

Survival

The survival tradition arose primarily among the plantation slaves as a spiritual antidote to their terrible suffering. It was a natural expression of their dogged refusal to resign their personhood in the face of constant and systematic dehumanization. It is reflected in the puzzled reports of White missionaries who speak of the exoticism of the slaves' religious behavior—their love of conjuration, various forms of magic, voodoo and hoodoo (or more properly, neo-African religions like *vodun* and *obeah*), and other so-called corruptions of the religions of West Africa. These neo-African religions were a mixture of beliefs and practices brought mainly from areas known as Angola, the Congo, Nigeria, Dahomey, Togo, Ghana, and Gambia.

Reverend Charles C. Jones, the missionary responsible for the spread of the Presbyterian Church among slaves in Georgia, referred to these tendencies as "various perversions of the Gospel" and, in terms of the obstacles they presented to young, inexperienced missionaries, compared them to the product of "cultivated minds . . . of critics and philosophers."[1] In other words, these slaves knew what they were doing. They were trying, as best they could, to overcome the sheer absurdity of their condition. They erected, out of their African cultural and religious background, a bulwark against a dehumanizing experience cloaked in the sanctimonious pretensions of their oppressors. They attempted, against tremendous odds, to survive the false Christian teaching and brainwashing that was an obvious tool of their enslavement.

Liberation

The liberation subtradition, on the other hand, suggests a physically and psychologically more tolerable situation. It is reflected in sermons, legislative petitions, and various writings as the restiveness of people who seem to have survived the worst that slavery could do to them and now were moving on to a new stage—one demanding greater personal and political freedom. Although some slave churches in the South soon developed this rebellious spirit *sub rosa*, the liberation tradition in Black religion was most pronounced in the free Black communities of the North. Its emphasis was on breaking the chains of slavery that bound family members and friends who remained in the South and on protesting the discrimination and disabilities that those who had escaped or had been manumitted were experiencing in Baltimore, Philadelphia, New York City, and other cities of the North and West.

David Walker's Appeal: To the Coloured Citizens of the World of 1829 is an example of a document written by a free Black who was imbued with this liberation tradition.[2] The *Appeal* is an attack on White evangelical Christianity in the name of an evolving African American Christianity that began with the assumption that human liberation is at the heart of the gospel.

Elevation

The elevation subtradition is so close to the liberation position that from one perspective both subtraditions seem to be almost identical. However, in analyzing the response of the African American church to its environment, it is useful to distinguish between the general longing of the oppressed masses to throw off their bonds and strike for immediate political freedom, and a more precisely middle-class tendency that emphasized the role of religion in lifting African Americans up by their bootstraps—a disciplining, refining impulse found in the literature and organizing work of certain leaders. Its emphasis is on personal and social elevation—upon education, morality, and cultural "advancement"—rather than either sheer survival or immediate voting rights and other forms of political liberation.

A classic statement of the elevation motif is found in the old Spiritual "We Are Climbing Jacob's Ladder," which meant, among other things, ascending out of slavery, immaturity, and degradation toward a better, more respectable, and progressive future among the other races of the world. Elevationism is also expressed in the words of Bishop R. R. Wright of the AME Church when he described the founding principles of African Methodism. The purpose of the AME Church, the bishop said, is "among other things, to exemplify in the black man the power of self-reliance, self-help by the exercise of free religious thought with executive efficiency."[3]

A Complex Relationship

All these tendencies, or traditions, in African American religion were focused in different ways on freedom, and for that reason they interact with and interpenetrate each other in the complex history of African American Christianity in the United States. The survival tradition contained elements in closest approximation to the African inheritance. It was originally rural, lower class, pragmatic, and sometimes—like Job's wife—unabashedly irreverent. The liberation tradition was more urbane. At first it was encouraged by the genteel ideology of White men like Benjamin Lundy, William Lloyd Garrison, and other northern antislavery advocates and philanthropists. Ultimately, it became more prone to strategic political maneuvering and even to violence as a last resort. One hears it loud and clear in the famous 1843 address of Rev. Henry Highland Garnet, a Presbyterian, calling the slaves of the South to revolt. The elevation tradition was also characteristic of the aspiring middle-class mulatto communities in the North and the South, but it was less interested in the bravado of political agitation and rather more responsive to the counsel of southern spokespersons like Booker T. Washington than to fiery northern liberationists like W.E.B. Du Bois.

It is important to note that the survival tradition, in the desperate struggle to keep Black folk alive, sought whatever was available to sustain life and sanity. Where external freedom was difficult or impossible to secure, it relied on internal or psychological freedom—hence the emotional displays of spirit possession, the prayer bands, and the ring shouts that proper ecclesiastics like John Chavis, an early Black Presbyterian preacher, and Daniel A. Payne, a bishop of the AME Church, deplored. The liberationists, of course, sought the external freedom that their longing eyes could see rising on the horizon of the times. They were inspired by the ideals of the American Revolution and the White antislavery movement around New York City and Philadelphia—both, not surprisingly, becoming centers of Black religious rebellion. The liberation tradition was not focused so much on coping strategies, on staying alive under the brutality of the system, but on fighting boldly for freedom from chattel slavery and from White supremacy over the bodies and souls of Black men and women. The elevation tradition sought freedom from ignorance, immorality, and degradation of every kind. Its concern was not so much staying alive or obtaining immediate political relief, but achieving an ennobling respectability and all the recognized marks of civilization—bringing the African American community under the discipline of industry, temperance, modesty, frugality, and the kind of personal and cultural proprieties that would earn it the esteem and admiration of all people of good will.

W.E.B. Du Bois was the first to recognize these variant strands of Black religion, although he does not attempt to classify them as subtraditions. In his masterpiece *The Souls of Black Folk*, Du Bois speaks of two types of religion: one "that became darker and more intense," that included a note of revenge that was pessimistic about life—"a complaint and a curse, a wail rather than a hope, a sneer rather than a faith." Here is a strong intimation of what we are calling the survival tradition. He also speaks of a religion among Blacks that is shrewd and optimistic, not above compromise or even hypocrisy, endeavoring "to turn [the White man's] weakness to the black man's strength."[4] Here it is possible to discern an aspect of what we are calling the liberation motif or tradition.

Du Bois does not attempt to isolate an elevation tradition, perhaps because he could not name what he sensed to be his own weakness—a secret enchantment with European civilization—and found himself torn between fostering elitism and agitating for a liberationist stance. Nevertheless, he seems to have differentiated between at least two kinds of responses of African American practitioners of religion to their condition in America. He recognized the importance of the emphasis on self-reliance and elevation in Washington's view, but would give it a more sturdy political relevance and make it a part of what we are calling the liberation tradition.

After emancipation, the relationship between these seminal strands of Black religiosity became more ambiguous because they became more and more intertwined. In one sense they continued to be observable in the distinction E. Franklin Frazier made between the "invisible institution" of the slave church in the South and the "visible institution" of the church of the freed men and women of the North. But after the Civil War a more complicated picture arises. There is a sense in which the liberation and elevation subtraditions, subtly modified by the sterner religiosity of the rural folk who migrated to the urban North, came to dominate the masses of churchgoing Negroes. Under the impact of the Great Migration, the focus of African American Christianity shifted to an emphasis upon internal spiritual freedom that preserved the influence of African spirituality while, at the same time, it continued to resist the massive destruction of personality and community that characterized what polite conversation called "the previous condition of servitude." The mainline African American churches, including Presbyterian congregations, partially absorbed and domesticated elements of the survival tradition of the folk, but they also attempted to fend off the "Africanisms" and other more "folksy" characteristics of the storefront churches. By the beginning of the twentieth century, the mainstream of African American Protestantism began to look more and more like its White counterpart.

Sectarian and Cultic Black Religion Revived

The earlier, "lower-class" survival tradition, however, was never completely eradicated from the African American community. The conditions of African American life in the city were too precarious for that to happen. Rather, it lived on in new religious groups that sprang up in the ghettos and rural slums, North and South. A survivalism, more sophisticated than when William Wells Brown said he was enchanted by Dinkie, the hoodoo man, or when the AME bishops railed against "cornfield ditties" masquerading as Methodist hymns, stirred impatiently in the souls of the masses. It was to break out most vociferously in Black Holiness and Pentecostalism, and various other explosions of popular religiosity. Garveyism is the best example of the survival tradition institutionalized. After that we can trace its development from the 1920s, intricately intermeshed with the liberation tradition, through the period of civil rights and finally to what Vincent Harding called "the religion of Black Power" that arose in the late 1960s.[5]

We must not miss the significance of the urban sects and cults. They revitalized and redirected the survival tradition of the folk by infiltrating some of the mainline Black churches. They kicked open old doors and broke through new ones that allowed certain forms of African, Native American, Asian, and Judaic spirituality to infuse Negro Christianity. Some of this creativity and openness to unfamiliar religious ideas seeped into the mainstream; but because the liberation and elevation subtraditions continued to dominate the older, White-influenced interpretations of the faith, the churches of the middle class were never able to be as doctrinally and liturgically pure as Bishop Daniel Payne and other churchmen would have wished.

Thus a considerable part of the African American religious experience has diverged from the theological and liturgical trajectory of the White churches. That should not surprise us. African American Christianity at all levels had to wrestle with questions and come up with answers with which White Christianity, generally speaking, had no commerce. Ours was, first and foremost, a religion of a poor and oppressed class of people who were regarded scarcely as human by White society. It was also a religion that veered from the central tradition because its roots were in sub-Saharan Africa rather than Europe. Although much of this inheritance has evaporated from African Methodism and the Black congregations that belong to the predominantly White denominations, enough of it is still clinging to churches at the lower end of the socioeconomic spectrum at the dawn of the twenty-first century to give a definite flavor to the religion of the masses of African Americans. It is for this reason that most African American believers, for some years to come, will have no problem understanding what is meant when they hear this genre of Christianity referred to as Black or African American, despite strong tendencies in Scripture and the ecumenical movement to move us toward a church that knows no racial, gender, cultural, or class divisions.

Nevertheless, there are other considerations we need to make before plunging into the waters of that restless sea called Black Presbyterianism.

The Same Yet Different

What is it—this indefinable quality of Christian religion as practiced among African Americans today? Is it a certain lilt of music to which the sensuous body on Saturday night, as much as the sanctified soul on Sunday morning, cannot help but respond? Is it the way the choir marches down the aisle singing "We've Come This Far by Faith"—with that little half-step that looks as if it might break out at any moment into a holy dance to an unholy beat? Is it the way the Bible is interpreted in colorful word pictures as the preacher "tells the story" or sings it? Is it the way the Holy Ghost falls upon a congregation and can have folks laughing and crying at the same time—waving their arms in the charged air and calling out "Amen" and "Thank you, Jesus"? Can it be the traditional counterclockwise promenade every Sunday to the offering table, or the deacons' informal devotional period of "lining out hymns" before the pastor comes in, or the tiptoeing out to the restroom during the sermon with one finger pointed upward or the rich poetry of the spirituals and all that talk about "goin' home" and "Glory Land" in the gospel songs?

But then on a more cognitive level: Could it be a persistent belief in direct communication with God and the assurance that, according to a well-known folk saying, "He may not come when you want Him to, but He's always on time"? Is it an openness to doctrine that "feels right" to the community rather than conforms to some canon of orthodoxy? Could it be an eagerness to use the church for winning elections as well as winning souls—an assumption that religion has to do with *all* of life and a refusal, therefore, to draw any hard line between the sacred and the profane, the religious and the secular?

All of these characteristics and others that must go unexamined here for lack of space give the traditional African American devotional style a distinctive ambience and demeanor that distinguishes it from both White Protestant fundamentalism and White conservative evangelicalism. The church is still a primary expression of the Black personality despite the fact that today other institutions challenge its leadership. But even they are tottering on weak legs these days. The church remains the last bastion of the ethnic particularity of the African American community in the United States, combining in a variegated tapestry of older and newer ideologies, mythologies, attenuated cultural symbols and roles, perceptions of reality and patterns of behavior, all those hard-to-define elements that add up to what it means to be Black in this country—that mysterious quality of Christian identity that is the same and yet so different from the standard brand of the Christian faith.

What About the Oneness of the Church?

Of course, most African American churchgoers are not aware of these differences. Nor does all of this mean that there is no place for interracial and multicultural denominations and congregations in the United States. We are simply recognizing the fact that given the traditional roles and functions of African American churches in this society, it is not likely that they will fold up their tents and quietly fade into oblivion any time soon.

We will probably have a mixed scene in the foreseeable future. That is to say that African American churches will continue to exist across town and across the street from racially integrated churches that are trying to live out the mandate of Gal. 3:28: "There is no longer Jew or Greek, there is no longer slave or free, there is no longer male and female; for all of you are one in Christ Jesus." But it may well be that these racially integrated and multicultural congregations will be the poorer, liturgically and otherwise, if they are not able to draw some of their sustenance from the wellsprings of the distinctive spiritual dynamism that has been nurtured for so many years in America's Black churches—churches that also yearn for the visibility of the "one holy catholic and apostolic church," but have a vague sense of being different even as they strive to be the same.

African American Christianity Defined

After all we have been saying about the indefinable qualities of African American religion, it may seem odd to venture to define it. But before going on to examine Black Presbyterianism, we should at least suggest a definition of African American Christianity, the spirit and traditions of which African American Presbyterians share.

However, we must be very clear about one thing. The usefulness of definitions is not that they settle something once and for all, but that they give us a starting point for examining reality and trying out various ways of understanding it. What follows below is not the end of the study of African American Christianity but the beginning. Our definition is a tentative, experimental model that will lend itself to further discussion and research.

The term *Black Christianity* is sometimes used by scholars to refer to the Christian religion as practiced by all people of African descent—whether on the continent of Africa or in the Diaspora. Here we use the term interchangeably with African American Christianity to refer more precisely to the present dominant form of religion in the Black, or African American, communities of North America. Thus we can define Black Christianity as the particular appropriation that African Americans made of a traditional belief in God that originated in Africa prior to the coming of White men, including the ancient African church of the upper Nile Valley, and to which, in a real sense, they were reintroduced in the form of a Europeanized and Americanized form of Christianity by White missionaries in colonial America.

This appropriation is the same yet different from Christianity as practiced by most Caucasians in Europe and North America. It has lost but is trying to regain some values of the ancient Africanization of Christianity in Ethiopia and Nubia that made its own distinctive contribution to the catholic faith in the early centuries of Christian history, but it continues to reflect, however partially and dimly, a West African religious and cultural inheritance together with the intense experience of God during slavery that combined form the basic groundwork of its present worldviews and traditions.

In the first two chapters of this book we have identified some of those major views and traditions and have seen how they both shaped and were shaped by historical developments in the United States. We need to take special note of one particular development in response to our environment that has made all the difference—the quest for freedom and antiracism.

Black Christianity reflects most clearly the historic struggle against racism and oppression that African Americans have tried to understand and oppose through the gospel of Christ. The determination to be free, therefore, is at the core of this way of being Christian and is expressed in many ways: music, modes of worship, styles of preaching and public prayer, ethical commitments and beliefs about social justice, and in what many believe about the nature of Deity and the immediacy of Deity's claim on the creation and humankind.

African American Christianity is characterized on the one hand by a deep spirituality—highly personal and emotional—and on the other hand by a hard-nosed, pragmatic approach to reality that is strongly communal and political in its orientation. Some of this kind of Black religion may be disappearing today, but it is still pronounced in many congregations that are affiliated with the historic Black denominations. But this peculiar African American approach to the Christian faith is also found, with increasing frequency since the Civil Rights revolution, in Black and racially integrated congregations that continue to be a small but vocal minority within the predominantly White churches of the United States, including Roman Catholicism.

Let us now see what this African American Christianity looks like in one particular constituency of a predominantly White Protestant denomination—

the Presbyterian Church (U.S.A.). In doing so we will have to ask why some Black people, until now, have insisted on remaining in this church, why some are now considering a proposal to separate from it, and what it means—at least from the point of view of this book—to be an African American Presbyterian today.

Questions for Discussion

Scripture for Reflection: James 3:1–5

1. Discuss the primary focus of each subtradition that developed in African American religion. Cite any examples of these traditions operating simultaneously today.

2. When were African Americans first introduced to the concept of worshiping a supreme God? Discuss your findings.

3. Is it heretical for African Americans to implement African culture, history, and spirituality into our worship and study experiences?

4. W.E.B. Du Bois had a secret enchantment with European civilization and found himself torn between fostering elitism and agitating for a liberationist stance. Are there any similarities between Du Bois and twentieth-century African American Presbyterians?

5. Would a European church that sincerely welcomes African American members represent a closer move toward a universal church that knows no racial, gender, cultural, or class divisions?

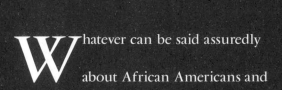

Whatever can be said assuredly
about African Americans and
Presbyterianism, they do not seem to
embrace each other comfortably.

3   African Americans and the Presbyterians

If it is difficult to define African American Christianity, try to define African American Presbyterianism! In light of what we have said about the African American Christian's connection to his or her African cultural roots, about the emotional content of Black religion, its pragmatic spirituality and its obsession with freedom from racism and other kinds of human oppression, nothing would seem more unlikely than to find Black religion combined with the cool, unornamented, duty-bound religion of Euro-American Presbyterianism.

"Black Presbyterians?" a Baptist seminarian in Atlanta once quipped. "Isn't that what they call an oxymoron?" He was not very far off his target. A familiar allegation in the African American community is that if you happen to run into a Black Presbyterian, "somebody has probably been messing around with his or her religion!"

On the other hand, these comments ought not be taken too seriously. The Reformed or Presbyterian tradition was originally much concerned with freedom from the tyranny of civil power and resistance to all forms of religious oppression. The true followers of John Calvin had a guilty conscience about the treatment of the poor and other kinds of social injustice. Despite the deplorable record of some of their churches in America on the slavery question, they found it difficult to shrug off a sense of responsibility for doing something about it.

Yet we have to concede that, taken as a whole, Anglo-Saxon Presbyterianism is about as close a cousin to the Black religious experience as "Annie Laurie" by the Royal Bagpipes of Scotland is to "Body and Soul" by Fats Domino.

Whatever can be said assuredly about African Americans and Presbyterianism, they do not seem to embrace each other comfortably. In the 1960s, during the United Presbyterian Ministers' Project in Hattiesburg, Mississippi, although there were White southern Presbyterians in the same town, not only did some of the Black folks have difficulty pronouncing our church's name, but they found it incredible that there were people of their own color in the North who called themselves "Pedestrians."

Little did they know that there were African American families in the Carolinas and Georgia whose membership in the Presbyterian Church went back more than six generations, or that in Philadelphia the First African Presbyterian Church has had an uninterrupted existence for one hundred and ninety years!

Almost from the beginning of the Presbyterian Church in America, there have been people who could be described figuratively as "Afro-Saxon Presbyterians"; they accepted only trained ministers and were proud that their children could recite the Shorter Catechism and quote long passages from the Westminster Confession. African American Presbyterians stick out their chests over Lucy Craft Laney, a slave woman who founded a pioneering Black school in Augusta, Georgia, and Daniel Jackson Sanders, who was also born in slavery and became a scholarly southern Presbyterian minister after the Civil War. He was the first African American president of Biddle University (now Johnson C. Smith University) in Charlotte, North Carolina. The name of Albert Byron McCoy is also revered among African American Presbyterians in the South. McCoy was for many years the director of Sunday school missions in the North Carolina heartland of African American Presbyterianism.

Leaders like these remind us that, despite the young seminarian's cynical remark, there have always been African Americans who had no doubt that Presbyterianism was just as natural for them as it was for any Scotch-Irish immigrant in Pittsburgh or Richmond. They were proper Presbyterians in every sense of the word, imbued with a zeal for elevation, and they would be offended by any suggestion that this refined form of Euro-American Protestantism did not befit their religious sensibilities better than any other they knew about.

These considerations, however, do not change the fact that Presbyterianism, as transplanted in North America, was at a severe disadvantage in comparison with the Baptists and Methodists when it came to appealing to the slaves and taking sides with them against the "peculiar institution." In those more "evangelical" churches, the Africans found greater freedom of worship under their own leaders, a more easily understood doctrine, and more consistent opposition to slavery. The Black Methodists were particularly impressed with those features of Wesleyanism in the eighteenth century.

In order to begin at the beginning, let us set the Presbyterian churches in the larger context of the history of Western Christianity. Where did these dour, White people come from in the first place? Who were the first Presbyterians, and what did they believe?

A System of Church Government

The first thing we have to recognize is that Presbyterianism has to do with church government. Presbyterians believe that their form of the church goes back to New Testament times when the apostles installed in each church two groups of leaders. One group performed acts of rulership and were called presbyters or elders. A second group, who were called deacons, comfortably performed acts of service and charity. (See Acts 14:23; Titus 1:5; and Acts 6:1–6, although the term *deacon* is not used in the latter scripture passage.) According to this practice, the pastor was nothing more nor less than an elder who had been given teaching rather than explicitly ruling authority and was in charge of administering the Word (preaching) and the Sacraments (the Lord's Supper and Holy Baptism).

In sixteenth-century Europe, this form of church government was considered strictly biblical and was brought to the attention of some of the Reformers when they turned to Scripture rather than to Rome as the sole authority for determining how the church should be governed. A presbyterian form of church government was first introduced in Geneva, Switzerland, by John Calvin (1509–1564). It then spread to other Reformed churches throughout Europe.

Although *Calvinism* is commonly associated with Presbyterianism, in common parlance it refers to considerably more than a system of church government. Calvinism is essentially a cultural system and a school of theology that emphasizes the sovereignty and glory of God as the ground of all religious, social, and political life that is conformed to biblical revelation. It calls on believers to be totally dependent on the providential will of God in all things. The doctrine of predestination is frequently mentioned as the keystone of Reformed or Presbyterian theology, although today most Presbyterian denominations have modified its original severity in the interest of modern sensibilities.

But as important as theology is to Presbyterians, it would be correct to say that Presbyterianism (as opposed to Calvinism) refers less to a religious worldview or plan of salvation than it does to a particular form of church government—rule by presbyters at local, regional, and national levels through the instrumentality of an equal number of teaching (ministers) and ruling elders (lay men and women elected to represent the congregation) rather than by a council of bishops or other ecclesiastical overseers.

We cannot let ourselves get involved here in a discussion of the doctrinal basis of Calvinism, but a few more comments are in order to help us to put Presbyterianism, prior to the conversion of African slaves in the American colonies during the seventeenth and eighteenth centuries, in its proper historical setting.

Puritanism, Presbyterianism, and Revolution

During the sixteenth century, King Henry VIII of England succeeded in establishing what was essentially a Roman Catholic church in England, except that it was independent of Rome. The Church of England defiantly refused to recognize the pope but left many of the doctrines and rites of standard Roman Catholicism intact. By the time Elizabeth I took the throne in 1558, many English people had been won over to the model of a theocratic state such as John Calvin and other Reformers had created in Geneva. With this in mind, the most radical Protestants were impatient with Elizabethan Anglicanism and sought to purify it by discarding all marks of Roman Catholicism and returning to what the continental Reformers believed were the characteristics of the New Testament church.

Among these Puritans were people called Presbyterians. They formed the first English presbytery as early as 1572 and refused to conform to the Church of England. They were, however, less radical than their fellow Puritans, who called themselves Congregationalists or Independents and desired a Church of England in which every local congregation would govern itself. The Presbyterians, on the other hand, wanted government by presbyteries, or groups of teaching and ruling elders from several congregations located in the same geographical area.

After Elizabeth's death in 1603, the Presbyterian Puritans continued to be persecuted by King James VI of Scotland, who succeeded the Queen as James I of England. The obsession of Puritanism for a culture, church, and state totally anti-Catholic and governed by the "pure morality of the Bible" led inevitably to revolution. Throughout this period Presbyterians had little to say about slavery in the colonies but a great deal to say about what vestments English clergy should wear in the pulpit and what liturgy should be used for divine worship.

Charles I, who succeeded his father, James I, was not disposed to tolerate their nonsense and harried the Puritans, including Presbyterians, out of England and finally into the "howling wilderness" of North America. For his pains he was finally executed in 1649 after civil war had ravaged his kingdom for seven years. In the meantime, Presbyterians were among those who founded the Massachusetts Bay Colony in 1630 and had begun planting churches in the New World. Back in England, the doctrines of Puritanism had been systematized and promulgated by the Westminster Assembly of ministers and laymen who met from 1643 to 1649 by order of Parliament. The Parliament voted to make use of the Assembly's advice on what the final reformation of the Church of England should look like.

What is called the Westminster Confession became the official creed of Presbyterians and the most influential pronouncement of Protestant theology in the seventeenth and eighteenth centuries. Not only was it authoritative for all Presbyterians, but Congregationalists and many Baptists adopted the Westminster Confession, with certain omissions and additions, as the substance of doctrine taught in the Scriptures. The original Confession comprised thirty-three articles with proof texts bearing on what has generally been recognized as the five points of Calvinism: divine sovereignty, human depravity, limited atonement, irresistible grace, and the perseverance of the saints. But this is not the place to discuss those doctrines. Suffice it to say that today most Presbyterian churches hold to more contemporary statements of faith while believing that they are based generally on the Westminster Confession.

It was the intention of those who formulated the Confession that Presbyterianism would become the accepted form for the Church of England. However, Oliver Cromwell, the dangerously self-righteous leader of the civil war, opposed Presbyterianism. As a result, Congregationalism, which held that neither bishop nor presbytery should have authority over the local congregation, became the order of the day. As it turned out, Presbyterian churches never gained a firm foothold in England and indeed found themselves in strong competition with Congregationalism and other forms of dissent in the American colonies.

Presbyterianism was, nevertheless, viable enough in Scotland and Wales, and through the immigration of many of its adherents to America it became one of the most powerful representations of Protestantism in the world. American Presbyterians organized their first presbytery in 1706, and their potential for radicalism is seen in the fact that they were among the most enthusiastic supporters of the revolution against England. The representative form of government adopted by the Continental Congress was partly influenced by the Presbyterian form of church government. The high educational standards of Presbyterian clergy and the explicit ideas they had about freedom and morality contributed to the dominant role the denomination played throughout the Revolutionary War period and into the nineteenth century.

How Presbyterians Related to African Americans

It is during the period leading up to the Revolution of 1776, called by some in those days "the Presbyterian rebellion," that we pick up the emergent relationship between White Presbyterians and the African American population of colonial America. It was slow in coming. Already, by the middle of the sixteenth century, most learned Whites must have known that there were Black men and women being snatched from Africa and enslaved by White Christians for a lifetime of hard labor in the Spanish and Portuguese possessions of the New World. Yet we search in vain to find where the Westminster Confession or any of the eminent theologians of the Reformation took much notice that the renunciation of "manstealing" was a reasonable requirement to lay on any pious Protestant. It is interesting, in this regard, that John Knox (1514–1572), a Scottish Reformer and the second great figure of Presbyterian history, waxed so enthusiastically about Calvin's Geneva that he called it "the most perfect school of Christ that ever was on earth since the days of the apostles."[1] He did not mention, however, that the curriculum did not include the moral abhorrence that biblically enlightened Christians ought to feel toward chattel slavery.

Good Presbyterian dons could be greatly exercised over church government and what to wear in the pulpit, but it took two hundred years from the days of Calvin and Knox for a General Assembly of their church to condemn slavery. Even that first definitive statement, made after hot debate in 1818, was weakened by qualifications and applied no sanctions against church members and ministers who held slaves. In 1858, one of the smaller Presbyterian churches, the United Presbyterian Church of North America, bravely declared that slavery was "a violation of the law of God and contrary both to the letter and spirit of Christianity."[2] But until the Civil War, the vast majority of Presbyterians could own slaves without any body of church law or doctrine telling them that they were committing a sin.

By comparison, the Methodists did not appear until the middle of the eighteenth century, but under their leaders, John Wesley and Thomas Coke, Methodists did much more for the cause of antislavery in the colonies. Some early Methodists in the West Indies and in North America held slaves, but they knew that their "society" and many of their preachers condemned the practice on theological and ethical grounds.

The Baptists split in 1845 over the slavery question after having earlier spun off antislavery churches like the "Emancipating Baptist" congregations in Virginia and Ohio that made the abolition of slavery a basic tenet of their faith.

The Evangelization of Presbyterian Slaves

According to Rev. W. H. Franklin, a Presbyterian educator who wrote *The Early History of the Presbyterian Church in the U.S.A. Among the Negroes,* the first Black slaves were introduced to Presbyterianism while working in the homes of pious White Presbyterians. There they were taught to read and memorize passages from the Shorter Catechism and the Bible. During the eighteenth and nineteenth centuries, many Whites believed that the words of Ps. 68:31 were being fulfilled by their evangelical zeal for the souls of Black folk. Black people of the world were "stretching out their hands to God" by being converted, and their masters should do what they could to provide for the salvation of their "Ethiopians" (Acts 8:26–40), who were destined to return to Africa and do the same for their benighted brethren.

Franklin tells us that these pious White Presbyterians began with the children. African American children were often taught in the plantation big house by the young White children of slaveholders. More formal instruction was done in the churches after the White service.

> They attended many Sabbath schools with the white people and were taught at the same time and place or in the afternoon. If the colored children had their Sabbath school in the afternoon, they were taught by the white members of the church. This is why the slaves and servants coming from Presbyterian homes showed superior intelligence.[3]

As we have already learned, the first organized Presbyterian effort to reach the slaves was initiated in 1747 by Rev. Samuel Davies, a "New Side" (or revivalistic, though modified, Calvinist) Presbyterian minister. Davies preached in Virginia, and from his labors the Hanover Presbytery developed, which included most Presbyterian congregations south of the Potomac River. Ten years later, in 1757, Davies reported that he had baptized some 150 slaves and commented further on his opinion that the care of the souls of Black slaves was "an awful and important trust"[4] from God. It was not until 1789 that the first Presbyterian General Assembly was held on American soil and the topic of slavery began to be debated in this highest judicatory of the church. Although a few colonial clergy and laymen openly opposed slavery, the Presbyterian Church as a whole, with its influential constituency in the Carolinas, put its emphasis on the "religious instruction" of the slaves rather than their immediate emancipation.

The hard fact is that the class-conscious Presbyterians were more prejudiced against Blacks than either the Methodists or the Baptists. None of the White churches did anything to crow about, but both of the latter denominations made a bolder effort than the followers of John Calvin to rid themselves of slaveholders and bring the Black converts into their congregations. One of the consequences was that both the Baptists and the Methodists attracted a larger number of slaves to their services than did the Presbyterians, and throughout the history of this country those two denominations have been more intimately known and regarded more favorably by African Americans.

There was an elitism about the racism of many Presbyterian clergy. At a meeting of the Synod of Virginia in 1867, Rev. Robert L. Dabney, arguing against granting ecclesiastical equality to African American preachers in the southern Presbyterian Church, made a statement that illustrates the arrogance and self-delusion on the race question among some White Presbyterians.

> I oppose the entrusting of the destinies of our Church, in any degree whatsoever, to black rulers, because that race is not trustworthy for such position. There may be a *few exceptions*: (I do not believe I have ever seen one, though I have known Negroes whom I both respected and loved, in their proper position) but I ask emphatically, Do legislatures frame general laws to meet the rare exceptions? or do they adjust them to the general average?[5]

All African American ministers and lay commissioners from local Black congregations experienced discrimination at meetings of presbyteries, and some bitterly complained about it. Rev. Samuel Cornish, an African American clergyman of the Presbyterian Church U.S.A. (the so-called northern church), wrote:

> I have seen a minister of Jesus Christ sitting in Presbytery, with his white brethren in the ministry, who, though it had been announced that full provision was made among the church members for every brother . . . yet [was] left by himself in the church for three successive days, without dinner or tea, because no Christian family could be found in the congregation who would admit him to their table, on account of his color.[6]

The race question first came up in the Presbyterian Church in 1774. From that year until the Civil War divided the denomination North and South, no church was more high-sounding and profound in its biblical and theological analysis of slavery or did less about it. Only a handful of embattled White Presbyterians dared to challenge the denomination to stop tolerating the presence of slaveholders in its membership. The church hemmed and hawed over the question, but it did not forthrightly support antislavery.

In 1797, when the Presbytery of Transylvania received the question "Is slavery a moral evil?" a vote was taken and the answer was "Yes." A second question was posed: "Are all persons who hold slaves guilty of a moral evil?" Another vote gave the answer as "No." This was understandable, considering the fact that some persons inherited slaves at the deathbed of a parent or spouse, some had given their slaves papers for their gradual emancipation, and others had even purchased slaves with the sincere intention of setting them free sometime after, and sometimes even before, they had worked off their purchase price.

But when a third question was put for a vote by the presbytery to force it to decide, if not *all* slaveholders were guilty of sin, which of them should be so considered, the answer came back: "Resolved that the question . . . be put off until a future day." The Presbyterian historian Professor Andrew E. Murray remarks dryly, "This day seems never to have arrived."[7]

The case of Rev. George Bourne, of Lexington Presbytery in Virginia, gives us another example of how the Presbyterian Church, in both the North and the South, skirted the issue of slavery with eloquent words and empty gestures. Because of Bourne's strong antislavery views, the Virginia slaveholders manufactured a charge against him and persuaded his presbytery to depose him. When his case was appealed to the 1818 General Assembly, the highest judicatory of the church, Bourne's deposition was upheld while at the same time the Assembly tried to save face by issuing a resounding antislavery resolution. Stung by its action, Bourne accused the Assembly of rank hypocrisy.

The antislavery resolution, which many southern commissioners voted for, he argued, was passed simply to satisfy the consciences of the northern and eastern churches in exchange for permitting the slaveholders of Virginia to unfrock him as a dangerous enemy of the denomination.

"They only intended by it," Bourne said of the northern churchmen who upheld his deposition while making an empty gesture against slavery, "to blind their eyes to the true character and wickedness of slavery, and to silence the outcry and disquietude respecting their being participants with their [the slaveholders'] guilt."[8]

African American Presbyterians must have watched this spectacle of pious fraud with little humor. It was becoming increasingly clear that the Presbyterian Church condemned slavery in theory but condoned it in practice. Ironically, the preaching and teaching ministry to African American members increased in inverse proportion to the church's refusal to adopt forthrightly the position of radical abolitionism. Darius L. Swann, in his excellent book *All-Black Governing Bodies: The History and Contributions of All-Black Governing Bodies,* writes:

> Notwithstanding the fervor (some would say fanaticism) of the abolitionists and the Jesuitical arguments of the pro-slavery adherents, the large body of Presbyterians, North and South, seemed simply to wish that the whole slavery issue would go away. When forced to face the issue they temporized. The Presbyterians acknowledged that slavery was an evil practice and not in accord with the tenets of their faith, but they could not bring themselves to declare that slavery was a sin. That would have required disciplinary action against slaveholders, which they had not found the courage to adopt.[9]

The more White Presbyterians tiptoed around the disciplining of slaveholding members, the more their consciences drove them to what they considered to be the next best thing—bringing the slaves to Jesus Christ through zealous religious instruction. In other words, evangelizing and doing good for the poor Black people became an acceptable substitute for demanding that the Presbyterians who held them in bondage set them free.

Of course, in nineteenth-century America, few White Christians were in a position to exceed the benevolence the Presbyterians showed toward their wards. Presbyterians, after all, were the backbone of the growing middle and upper classes. Their pastors and missionaries were the most learned in the nation and, therefore, could be of the greatest assistance to African American people who were constantly looking for opportunities to teach themselves how to read and write. In terms of educational ministries, the Presbyterian plantation missionaries were superior to the more enthusiastic though less erudite Baptist and Methodist missionaries. Anyone who is curious about why, notwithstanding the anemic position the Presbyterians took against slavery, some African Americans were nevertheless drawn to the church should probably look for the reason in the widely publicized educational ministries that Presbyterians offered Black people after slavery was abolished.

In addition to education, Presbyterian missionaries placed considerable emphasis on "decency and order"—or manners, personal morality, and refined group behavior. There is no doubt that some slaves, before the Civil War, and many freed men and women after it yearned to elevate themselves in both book learning and the proprieties of the White upper classes.

The First African Presbyterian Church of Philadelphia prided itself in sponsoring a day school that was supported by some of the most prestigious White families of the city. We should not be surprised to learn that in this congregation, according to one of its early pastors, "the claims of the Gospel . . . [were] addressed more to the conviction of the conscience and understanding of the people, than to the prejudices and passions." The Synod of New York and New Jersey established an African School in 1816 that continued with some difficulty for nine years. The earliest African American Presbyterian missionary, Rev. John Chavis, organized a school for both Whites and Blacks in North Carolina, despite laws throughout the South after 1831 that prohibited anyone from teaching slaves to read and write.

Nearly all African American Presbyterian pastors augmented their salaries by teaching. Relatively few Blacks in the North, and only a small percentage of the estimated seventy thousand slaves owned by Presbyterians in the South, answered the call to discipleship, but those who did may well have joined the church as much for educational and social betterment as for any other reason. It was a commonplace expectation that the sober-minded followers of John Calvin would put more stock in the enlightenment of the mind than in the shouting baptismal rites of the Baptists or the "strangely warmed heart"[10] of the Methodists.

Were the first African American Presbyterians duped into accepting the charity of the Presbyterian Church as a substitute for the difference the church's considerable resources might have made on the side of the struggle against slavery and racism? That is doubtful. It must have occurred to many of them that education and social status had limited value in view of the other disabilities they continued to suffer in both the North and the South. Moreover, although African American Presbyterians gladly accepted the ministries of the White church, they in fact did more to help themselves in the areas of education and cultural development than did their White patrons in their behalf. Another strategy was operating in this situation. What Blacks were prepared to do was to turn the intellectual weapons that White Presbyterians put in their hands against institutional racism in both the Presbyterian Church and the society.

None of their ministers illustrate this strategy during the antebellum period better than the two New York clergymen Samuel Cornish and Theodore S. Wright. These "coloured men," together with Henry Highland Garnet, J.W.C. Pennington, Lucy Craft Laney, Daniel J. Sanders, Francis Grimke, and others who labored in the three Presbyterian churches before the turn of the century, demonstrate the true spirit of Black Presbyterianism—to use every available resource of a trained mind, a committed soul, and a gentle spirit to uplift the race and hold constantly before the conscience of the White church the mandate of liberty and justice for all.

But let us look a little more closely at some of these African American Presbyterians who laid the foundation for what we call the Black Presbyterian heritage. This heritage should give us a justifiable pride in our past and an inextinguishable hope for the future.

Questions for Discussion

Scripture for Reflection: James 1:16–25

1. Is *African American Presbyterian* a contradiction in terms? Discuss your views.

2. Although it seems that African Americans and Presbyterians do not embrace each other comfortably, there have always been African Americans who had no doubt that Presbyterianism was just as natural for them as it was for their European brethren. Do African Americans remain in this denomination because it is comfortable, convenient, a means of escape, or a calling?

3. What are some of the advantages or blessings of being an African American Presbyterian?

4. How might a denomination whose roots are based on representation and equality—a denomination that experienced the hardship of religious persecution—be slow to speak out against the injustices of slavery and oppression?

5. Is there a link between the slaves and servants coming from Presbyterian homes showing superior intelligence and the false sense of superiority that African American Presbyterians feel over other Blacks today?

No study of the meaning and significance of Black Presbyterianism would be complete without at least a glance at the leaders of the resistance to slavery and racism that arose early among a few highly qualified and effective Black ministers who refused to relieve the pressure they put on the White church for change.

4   Pioneers of African American Presbyterianism

T here are too many early pioneers of Presbyterianism among African Americans for us to give them adequate attention in this small book. Beginning with John Chavis (1763–1838), the first African American to be licensed and ordained in the Presbyterian Church in 1801, and John Gloucester (1776–1822), the founder and first pastor of the First African Presbyterian Church of Philadelphia in 1807, many courageous men and women came forward in both the South and the North to give leadership to the small but growing number of Blacks who were being converted by the ministries of the three major American Presbyterian bodies: the Presbyterian Church U.S., or the "southern church" after the split in 1861; the Presbyterian Church in the U.S.A., or the "northern church"; and the United Presbyterian Church of North America, which had been formed in 1858 by the union of old Scottish Covenanter Presbyterians. The John Gloucester Memorial and Historical Society of Philadelphia, which has been collecting records and memorabilia for more than eighty-five years, is one of the research groups that can fill in the picture of what was happening in and around the First African Presbyterian Church in the early nineteenth century. Among the books and other resources cited in Resources for Further Study, special attention should be given to the aforementioned work of Darius L. Swann in the Report to the 205th General Assembly (1993) of the Presbyterian Church (U.S.A.) titled *All-Black Governing Bodies*, which contains a brief history of several early pastors and their congregations in the South. Swann's book is the first comprehensive study of the presbyteries and synods that were segregated judicatories of the three Presbyterian denominations prior to the mid-twentieth century.

Andrew E. Murray's *Presbyterians and the Negro*, published in 1966, and Inez Moore Parker's *The Rise and Decline of the Program of Education for Black Presbyterians of the United Presbyterian Church, U.S.A. (1865–1970)*, published in 1977, are two indispensable works that deal in fuller compass with the history of the African American pioneers in the building of churches and schools, two operations that were inseparable in the Presbyterian mission at home and in the foreign field.

The purpose of this chapter is to discuss the impact that some of the pioneers made on the ever-present race consciousness and fervor for social action that developed among African American Presbyterians over the years. No study of the meaning and significance of Black Presbyterianism would be complete without at least a glance at the leaders of the resistance to slavery and racism that arose early among a few highly qualified and effective Black ministers who refused to relieve the pressure they put on the White church for change.

Black Presbyterian Abolitionists

Samuel Cornish is best known in secular African American history as the editor of the first Black newspaper, *Freedom's Journal*. Cornish has the added distinction of being the founder of the First Colored Presbyterian Church of New York City in 1822. Rev. Cornish began his ministry as a missionary to indigent Blacks in the slums of lower Manhattan. His younger friend, Theodore S. Wright, was the first African American to graduate from a theological seminary, completing his studies at Princeton in 1828. Wright took over the New York congregation after Cornish and made it the second largest Black church in the city.

These two men were comrades-in-arms as far as the war against prejudice and discrimination was concerned. They stood side by side to represent the free Black community in the antislavery movement of the 1820s and 1830s, although Wright elected to remain in his church as a pastor rather than accept the invitation to go out on the circuit as an abolitionist lecturer.

Together Cornish and Wright attacked the segregated seating in White Presbyterian churches and chided their White brethren for so boldly denouncing slavery in the South while withholding civil rights from African Americans in the North. But neither Cornish nor Wright limited their protest activities to abolitionism and the integration of the lily-white structures of the Presbyterian Church. Although he remained a Presbyterian minister to the end, Cornish favored African Americans' attending their own churches, lest "they weaken the hands and discourage the hearts of their ministers by leaving them to preach to empty pews." His was a counsel of realism because it was certainly not expected that many Whites would attend African American churches. Neither Cornish nor Wright lowered his dignity by currying the favor of prejudiced Whites. In the 1840s Wright broke with his moderate

White friends by deliberately disobeying the law against giving assistance to fugitive slaves. He ignored the accusation of what today would be called reverse racism and the betrayal of White allies by urging African Americans to close their ranks, to organize politically and fight for the right to vote in New York State, rather than continue to depend on the eventual conversion of White people by moral suasion.

These two crusading ministers and their fellow African American Presbyterian clergy, like J.W.C. Pennington, Elymas P. Rogers, and Henry Highland Garnet, were not willing to drop quietly out of sight in the denomination, as many might have wished. Instead, they sought to fulfill their ordination vows as teaching elders by making the denomination face up to the gospel it proclaimed. In so doing, they emboldened both races to take more radical stances in the tumultuous years leading up to the Civil War. Wright was the mentor and inspirer of the famous Rev. Henry H. Garnet, whose powerful address in 1843 urged the slaves to throw down their rakes and hoes and begin an armed struggle for freedom. Garnet was a Presbyterian firebrand, and there were few abolitionists, including the redoubtable Frederick Douglass, who could match his passion for getting African Americans to stand on their own feet and do something about the liberation of the millions of their brothers and sisters still bound in fetters in the South.

The Mission to the Newly Freed People

The General Assembly, meeting in Pittsburgh on May 18, 1865, took action to dispatch missionaries, teachers, and material resources to the South to aid the newly emancipated people. It proved to be a decision that had inestimable consequences for the ingathering and elevation of African Americans by the northern Presbyterians, but it was a sword that cut two ways. It is quite likely that most of what has been right about the church's involvement with African Americans and most of what has been terribly wrong about that involvement have a common matrix in the policies and strategies adopted by the Freedmen's Board, the mission agency established for northern Presbyterian outreach to the ex-slaves. Although the number of African Americans who actually joined the northern church as a result of the missionary effort in the wake of the Union army was not impressive, the effect of the extensive network of Presbyterian parochial schools and colleges on the quality of African American life was extraordinary. Northern White men and women braved ostracism and even physical violence at the hands of embittered Confederates as they ministered to the freed people, many of whom had been members of the southern Presbyterian Church before 1861 but who had refused to go back to that denomination.

The missionaries of the Presbyterian Church in the U.S.A. (PCUSA) gave themselves sacrificially to the founding of churches, schools, and community projects throughout the states of the former Confederacy. The extent of the educational effort alone can be measured by the fact that as late as 1927 there were 19,000 African Americans enrolled in more than 160 Presbyterian schools and colleges—the vast majority in the South. The contribution of the church to the education of the Negro in the South, not only of Presbyterians, is without peer.

The Other Side of the Story

On the other hand, one finds a hint of the paternalism of some of these White missionary teachers in the statement of one of the field secretaries of the Freedmen's Board describing the familiar picture of the slave being lifted to his feet by the church: "Need we say the face of that prostrate helpless man is black? The strong beautiful hand reaching out to him is white."

Questionable presuppositions about what African Americans could and could not do for themselves, what they ought and ought not be taught in the church's schools; condescension about making them over into the image of White middle-class Presbyterians living in Pittsburgh and on the Philadelphia Main Line; and the unwillingness of the benefactors to turn over the control of the institutions and programs to Black leadership—all conspired to create unnecessary difficulties with which the Presbyterian Church is still contending.

Because of the inability of African Americans to fund their own work at adequate levels, they were forced to depend on the Freedmen's Board to pay their pastors' salaries and provide other aid to the fields. This not only created a feeling of abject dependency, which militated against good stewardship habits among African American Presbyterians, but also made it almost impossible for the all-Black governing bodies, the segregated presbyteries and synods, to exercise ecclesiastical authority over churches that were on the dole with the northern-based Freedmen's Board.

For example, as late as the 1940s Black Presbyterians were still faced with the problem of White control because of paternalistic policies put in place during Reconstruction by the Board. Clearly, the influence of the Freedmen's Board was not an unmixed blessing. In 1914 it even sought to supersede the regular Home Mission Board and take over all the work the denomination had with African American Presbyterians in the North. This was staunchly opposed by northern Blacks, but the all-White Board continued to administer missions among African Americans in the North and West as well as the South until 1923.

In a letter to his friend Dr. Francis J. Grimke, who was pastor of the Fifteenth Street Presbyterian Church in Washington, D.C., Rev. Matthew Anderson of Philadelphia reports the effort he made that year at the General Assembly to get the Freedmen's Board off their necks:

> I told them that the Overture which was passed in Rochester, practically turning all the work among colored people arbitrarily over to the Freedmen's Board, was seriously objected to by all the colored people of the north and by many of the white people also, and that we, the colored people, felt that it was simply a segregation of our churches, that it was drawing the color line, that it was a wet blanket upon all our work and that the colored churches in the north could not hope to succeed; that we did not want any special ecclesiastical legislation for our churches; that we wanted absolutely to have the same status that the white churches have.[1]

In a thrust for modernization, a Board of National Missions was created by the General Assembly, and within it, the Division of Work with Colored Persons—albeit, under a White administrator. African American Presbyterians were to experience some modicum of self-determination in the church by 1938 when Rev. Albert B. McCoy, a graduate of the seminary at Lincoln University, was elected the first Black to serve as secretary of a new unit responsible for the African American constituency. Although McCoy continued the paternalistic role of the church's mission program, he was able to open the doors for other pioneering African American field workers like E. J. Gregg, Frank C. Shirley, G. E. Casar, and Jesse Belmont Barber, in the four Black synods of the northern church.

Pioneers in the Overseas Mission

African American Presbyterians also made an important contribution to the Presbyterian mission overseas. Fifty-seven Black missionaries were sent by the northern church to its mission in Liberia between 1833 and 1891, but by the turn of the century only Whites were being appointed. Darius L. Swann writes:

> After considerable agitation, especially by Lincoln University students and a request by Catawba Synod to be assigned a parish in Africa to be supported by Catawba, the Board of Foreign Missions (PCUSA) indicated in 1927 its readiness to receive Black candidates for foreign mission service. In 1928, Irvin Underhill and his fiancée, Susan Theresa Reynolds, were appointed to serve in the Cameroons. When Underhill left the field in 1936, no other Blacks were appointed until 1948 when Darius L. Swann, a member of the Southern Virginia Presbytery, was sent to China to become the first African American to serve as a Presbyterian missionary in a non-African field.[2]

Two of the great pioneer foreign missionaries of the Presbyterian Church U.S. (PCUS) were William Henry Sheppard, Jr., and his wife, Lucy Gantt Sheppard. William Sheppard rose from being the sexton of the First Presbyterian Church of Waynesboro, Virginia, to become a distinguished graduate of Stillman College, the southern church's major school for Blacks in Tuscaloosa, Alabama, and an honoree of the Royal Geographical Society of London in 1893 for his explorations in the Kasai district of the former Belgian Congo, today the independent West African nation of Zaire.

After applying unsuccessfully to be appointed a missionary of the southern church, Sheppard was finally commissioned by the Foreign Mission Committee of the PCUS, becoming the first African American of that church to serve in Africa. He not only turned out to be one of the most powerful evangelists to work in the Congo, but with another missionary, John Morrison, he exposed to the eyes of the world, and then helped to abolish, the atrocious treatment of the Congolese people by King Leopold II of Belgium.

Blacks in the Presbyterian Church U.S. (PCUS)

The southern church disbanded its Committee on Colored Evangelization in 1911, but African American ministers were not to be given important positions in the church until 1945, when Lawrence W. Bottoms, the pastor of Grace

Presbyterian Church of Louisville, Kentucky, became the part-time Regional Director of Christian Education for the all-Black Snedecor Memorial Synod of the Presbyterian Church U.S. The southern church had taken half-hearted steps toward the creation of an independent Afro-American Presbyterian Church before the turn of the century, but when that ill-advised venture failed—partly because of the disinclination of key Black ministers and churches to join the proposed all-Black denomination—the Snedecor Memorial Synod was set up in its stead in 1917 and became the primary locus for the development of Black Presbyterianism in the church of the old Confederacy.

Bottoms became the Secretary of the Department of Negro Work, succeeding a White man, Alex Batchelor, in 1973. Bottoms had broken through the glass ceiling in several areas of the church's work prior to that time, serving as Assistant Secretary of the Division of Home Mission, Associate Secretary of the Division of Interpretation and Research of the Board of National Ministries, and Coordinator of Social Concerns in the early 1970s.

However, in both the northern and southern branches of Presbyterianism, the appointment of African Americans to the mission field and to high-sounding positions in the boards and agencies failed to change the basic pattern of paternalism or stem the tide of racism that continued to flow in the presbyteries and local congregations. It was well into the 1950s and 1960s before African American Presbyterians were able, through the militant politicking of race caucuses in both the northern and the southern church, to make their protest against blatant discrimination relatively effective, at least at the General Assembly level of the two denominations.

Black Presbyterian Solidarity through Caucuses

In face of long-standing problems with racial equality in both branches of the church, it is not difficult to understand why African American ministers chose to unite for concerted action. As early as 1893, Francis Grimke, R. H. Armstrong, Matthew Anderson, and John B. Reeve—four distinguished pastors of the northern church—founded the Afro-Presbyterian Council at the First African Presbyterian Church of Philadelphia. It was neither an idle gesture nor the first time that Black Presbyterian clergy had come together to arrogate their influence on the denomination. Informal caucusing had occurred among Black Presbyterian and Congregational clergymen even prior to the Civil War.

The Afro-Presbyterian Council proved to be expedient not only for political reasons but also because it provided a much-needed and regular opportunity for the fellowship and mutual edification that was hard for Blacks to come by in the "integrated" judicatories of the North. In the South, of course, Black PCUSA and PCUS clergy and laity were already involved with their respective constituencies in all-Black presbyteries and synods. Now the northern clergy had a formal organization that could represent the religious, social, and political interests of their members. In 1947 the name of the caucus was changed to the Council of the North and West, the dropping out of any racial designation suggesting the aspirations of African Americans in the North and West for total integration into the structures and programs of the denomination.

There was an occasion at the 1904 General Assembly to test the strength of the Afro-Presbyterian Council. The northern Presbyterians accepted an overture to seek union with the Cumberland Presbyterians, a White church that was strong in the mid-South and had expressed a desire to merge with other Presbyterian churches. But the Cumberlanders would not countenance interracial presbyteries, which would be the result of bringing the African American congregations that happened to reside within Cumberland bounds into existing White judicatories. African American leaders in the northern church indignantly opposed a Jim Crow Plan of Union, but the northern General Assembly approved the overture and created a Special Committee on the Territorial Limits of Presbyteries.

In its report, the committee recommended segregation, with the disingenuous observation about African Americans that "as a race they are inferior to the whites in culture, mental and moral development, and civilization; and for this reason they have a peculiar claim upon the stronger race for help and guidance."[3] But, of course, that help and guidance must of necessity come by way of separate congregations, presbyteries, and synods.

Dr. Grimke, whose church was one of the most prestigious congregations in Washington, D.C., led the Afro-Presbyterian Council in a valiant effort to turn back the merger proposal, but to no avail. The Black clergy, however, afterward used the caucus to empower the small minority of African Americans in the northern church, in spite of the de facto segregation that had been upheld by the 1905 decision to merge it with the Cumberland Church.

It was, however, a different and more far-reaching decision—the 1954 United States Supreme Court ruling that struck down "separate but equal"—that made a critical difference for the churches. The Brown decision embarrassed White Presbyterians and American Christian churches generally. The court emboldened African American Presbyterians and their allies to make a more determined effort to desegregate the church. In a burst of false optimism about the brotherhood and sisterhood they might expect in the immediate future, in 1957 the Council of the North and West agreed to disband and turn over its assets to the General Assembly, declaring that its usefulness had obviously come to an end in this long-awaited era of racial integration. It was an unfortunate miscalculation. The massive resistance to the Brown decision and to the Civil Rights movement generally, proved the optimism of the caucus to be premature.

Responses to the Civil Rights Movement

In 1964 African American Presbyterians began once again to organize. This time they created what was called Concerned Presbyterians, a more militant group, but again it left out of its name any indication of race consciousness. Edler G. Hawkins, Robert P. Johnson, Bryant George, Robert Shirley, and other activist clergy pressed the PCUSA to support the campaign of Dr. Martin Luther King Jr. by creating, at the highest level of the denomination, a Commission on Religion and Race (CORAR), with a half million dollar budget to thrust the church into the center of the struggle. The action of the Assembly was unprecedented.

At approximately the same time, Blacks in the PCUS were making a similar bid for power. In 1959 they set up their own organization—the Black Presbyterian Leadership Caucus (BPLC)—which sought unsuccessfully to link up with what had become by 1968 Black Presbyterians United (BPU), the revitalized caucus of the northern church. The BPLC, nevertheless, was able to leverage a certain amount of influence in southern Presbyterian structures and began to remove some of the obstacles that had prevented the White church from taking an advanced position on the Civil Rights movement and redressing the grievances of its African American members. Undoubtedly, some of the inspiration for the militancy of Blacks within the PCUS came from what they saw happening in the northern church.

Black Presbyterians United (BPU)

Five years after the Commission on Religion and Race was created at the Des Moines Assembly of the United Presbyterian Church in the United States of America (UPCUSA), many African Americans were radicalized by the new Black consciousness of urban grassroots movements in the North and West. At a national meeting in St. Louis, the newly rejuvenated Concerned Presbyterian caucus was scrapped for a deeper solidarity that more faithfully reflected the spirit and direction of African American Presbyterians in the 1960s. The new name was Black Presbyterians United (BPU). As one BPU brochure of the time put it: "The wall of segregation seemed as impregnable as ever, and there was little evidence that the church's practice was beginning to correspond with professions. There was much wrong in Zion!"

It was part of the strategy of the 1968 meeting that created BPU to push the younger and more aggressive leaders to the fore and for older, more moderate pastors and church executives, some of whom occupied key decision-making positions in the denomination, to line up behind them. Accordingly, Rev. E. Wellington "Tony" Butts, a young pastor from New Jersey, became the first BPU president. Immediately, Butts and his colleagues, who had been pressing for change, took over the reins with the full approval and protection of their elders. With youthful energy and uncompromising commitment to Black Presbyterian solidarity, countervailing power, and self-development, Butts led the new group in declaring, rather grandly:

> Black men and women must be enabled to significantly determine their lives and the nature of their communities. They must be free and able to respond to the forces that play upon their life. Black persons must have the opportunity to participate on an equal basis in all aspects of the larger pluralistic society and to work their will in the councils of nations and empires. To this end we seek power and for this purpose we bring this Black caucus into existence.

For all its grandiloquence, the statement represents an important turning point in the Presbyterian churches. Black Presbyterians, North and South, came of age in the 1960s after more than 150 years of uphill and downhill struggles within a denomination that always had difficulty matching intention with performance and overcoming the natural conservatism of great wealth and respectability.

We have not attempted to narrate the whole story of what African American Presbyterians accomplished or failed to accomplish during that long ordeal, but it is possible to see certain telltale attitudes and postures that we adopted. It is a story of movement out of a self-effacing innocence and gratitude to Whites for what African Americans had received from the Presbyterian churches, to the realization of the rich gifts we ourselves had brought to the churches and to the necessity of organizing for the requisite power to give those gifts greater visibility and clout in the life of the two major branches of American Presbyterianism.

Dr. Leland Stanford Cozart, the first African American president of Barber-Scotia College, wisely stated what had been the reality about Blacks and Presbyterianism since the two first encountered each other in the eighteenth century:

> Because of the Presbyterian Church, the Negro in America today is infinitely the richer in body, mind, and spirit; because of the Negro, the Presbyterian Church is immeasurably more responsive to human needs, more brotherly and more Christian.

Some Critical Questions

We must now turn to some of the weaknesses of African American Presbyterianism—weaknesses that sometimes grow out of a misunderstanding and misuse of the resources and opportunities God is making available to Black people at this important juncture in Presbyterian history. Even with the new sensitivity of the church to the fight against racism, there are temptations and miscalculations that we experience simply by being a part of a powerful, predominantly White, middle-class church in a world full of misery and injustice for most people of color.

How do African American men, women, and children find out who they really are in such a church as this and under such circumstances? How do they learn to appreciate our African and African American heritage without blowing both out of proportion and without separatist delusions?

How do they learn how to use power responsibly in order to make that heritage meaningful and useful in a pluralistic world? Can they discover how God wills to use the Black constituency to break down "the dividing wall of hostility" so that true reconciliation results from authentic liberation and the courage to unmask evil and challenge it without delusion and self-righteousness?

These are some of the questions we must now explore.

Questions for Discussion

Scripture for Reflection: James 2:14–26

1. Some critics of the Civil Rights movement argue that African Americans should not have fought to integrate but to build their own nation. With this paradigm in mind, do you believe that Black Presbyterian pioneers betrayed the Black masses by leading them into the racially unjust structures of the Presbyterian Church?

2. Is the responsibility of African American Presbyterians today to make the denomination face up to the gospel it proclaims?

3. If it pacifies but does not liberate, can the missionary work of the Presbyterian Church be compared to the statement "Christianity is the opiate of the people"?

4. Is it counterproductive to the cause of liberation for African American Presbyterians to seek permission from higher governing bodies to lift up the race?

5. How might Black Presbyterian caucuses be most effective in educating their European brothers and sisters while unifying African Americans in Black as well as predominantly White churches?

However, with respect to attitude, ambition, lifestyle, and the vision of a future for themselves and their children or grandchildren, most African American Presbyterians are solidly middle class.

5 Black Presbyterians and the Middle-Class Black Church

The African American Presbyterians belong, for the most part, to middle-class Black churches. This is not to say that our congregations are all full of stockbrokers, doctors, and businesspeople, or that the per capita income of the majority of the members would equal that of the average White congregation in a presbytery. In fact, the per capita income might exceed that of the average White congregation. Today in most Black families in the Presbyterian Church, both husband and wife are working full time, are burdened down with college loans, but, at the same time, are probably only one paycheck away from mortgage foreclosure.

However, with respect to attitude, ambition, lifestyle, and the vision of a future for themselves and their children or grandchildren, most African American Presbyterians are solidly middle class. We have a high regard for the same values—hard work, frugality, conventional morality, moderation in all things, higher education, patriotism, and godliness—that are professed by most Americans who live fairly comfortable and stable, albeit more and more stressful, lives in the great metropolitan centers of our nation.

African American preachers of all denominations like to talk about the poor and oppressed. Many of us think of ourselves as leading such people from Sunday to Sunday to ever more courageous sorties against the power and privilege of those who selfishly consume the largest proportion of America's goods and services. But the truth is that when most of the pastors of mainstream African American congregations look out from their pulpits on Sunday morning, they are looking at the haves rather than the have-nots. With some exceptions, most of us are ministering to well-fed, well-bred, well-groomed, and for the most part well-meaning people who, compared to the rest of the world and to some extent compared to a good percentage of the people around our churches, are middle class and proud of it. And if we're talking about Black Presbyterian congregations, we are probably too proud for our own good.

Over a period of several months in 1964, about three hundred Presbyterian ministers descended on Hattiesburg, Mississippi, where the Council on Church and Race of the UPCUSA had set up the headquarters of the

Hattiesburg Ministers Project. Physically, it was only a ramshackle office and a temporary dormitory in the Black community for housing visiting clergy from the North who spent several weeks in Mississippi assisting the local people to register and vote. Spiritually, it was a rare gift to an impoverished, demoralized town that was torn with racial strife and sorely needed a group of nonviolent, civil rights—committed Christians from the outside to work alongside the embattled coalition of local civil rights organizations that included the Student Nonviolent Coordinating Committee, the state NAACP, the Southern Christian Leadership Conference, and the Congress of Racial Equality.

Here at last, everybody said, was the Presbyterian Church "putting its body where its mouth was." The volunteers were mostly young White clergy who had answered the call from the new Council on Church and Race to take time away from their parishes up North to get involved where the civil rights battle raged the hottest. Day after day they canvassed the African American neighborhoods for prospective voters, walked picket lines in protest of the local officials who stubbornly refused to register Black voters, taught in emergency "Freedom Schools," and provided rural Mississippi, in various other ways, with a northern Presbyterian presence for several months. It was the Reconstruction Era all over again.

The Black folk of the area were overwhelmingly Baptist or members of a half-dozen strains of the Holiness and Pentecostal churches. They were poor dirt farmers and had little formal education. They and their ancestors had been the victims of the worst form of southern racism for generations. Many of them who joined with our ministers in the protest activity were particularly curious about those of us who happened to be the same color as they.

"I seed some White Pedestrians downtown," said one lady who provided additional housing for the project in her two-room tar-paper shack, "but I ain't never heard of no *colored* Pedestrians."

One of the pastors told her about the considerable number of African American Presbyterians who lived in the South. He suggested that there were even a few in Mississippi and that she ought to visit one of their churches sometime. Puzzlement darkened her broad, amiable face. She replied that although it wasn't her business, colored people were supposed to be either Baptist or Methodist.

"It ain't likely I'd be goin' to no Pedestrian church, Reverend," she said, "ya'll too high class fo' po' folks like me."

Some Erstwhile Fantasies about Black Presbyterians

The sister in Hattiesburg did not realize it, but she was voicing the opinion about Presbyterians held by many African Americans "too high class fo' po' folks," which is to say, for most Black folk. The opinion is not limited to people in the rural areas of the South. It was formerly and still is more than occasionally voiced by many African Americans in Atlanta, Charlotte, Philadelphia, and Chicago. But is it true? Or we might ask, is it *only* true as a fantasy of elitism that some African American Presbyterians would like to live up to this imagined elitism if they could?

The question calls to mind another belief about African American Presbyterians that is mixed up with the allegation that we are too snooty for most Black people. Some people begin by denying the appropriateness of even using the term *Black church* to refer to congregations that belong to predominantly White denominations like the Presbyterian, Episcopalian, Lutheran, or the United Church of Christ. They argue that not only do African American Presbyterians exhibit class characteristics that separate us from other Blacks, but that given the presbyterian form of government, our churches are under the control of a White majority. In their view, that is a most unfortunate state of affairs!

The going assumption is that only churches that are "owned and operated" by African Americans are free of White interference and can therefore call themselves a part of the Black, or African, American church in America.

There are, undoubtedly, some African American Presbyterians who are flattered to be regarded as part of a non-Black church and, as visitors used to report, lack the friendliness and warmth that is usually found in traditional African American congregations. Some African American Presbyterian churches want to give the impression that their services are "better," or "of a higher quality," or "more intellectual" than those of other churches. For many years there was a myth abroad that worship in African American Presbyterian churches was more "White" than "Black." But if that was ever true, it is important to recognize that the situation is rapidly changing today.

Most African American Presbyterian congregations may be a little more formal and lack some of the ardor of Black Baptists or Black Pentecostals, but Black Presbyterianism, as a subtradition, is a constituent part of whatever we mean by "the Black church tradition." Today the socioeconomic status of our members and the financial condition of our congregations are not so different from those of most AME or mainstream Baptist churches. Historically, African American Presbyterian churches cannot be separated from the so-called Black churches of America.

The First African Presbyterian Church of Philadelphia was founded before the city's first independent African American Baptist congregation and nine years before the Ecclesiastical Compact that created the African Methodist Episcopal Church. Although it had powerful White support, so did several other all-Black congregations in Philadelphia that were Baptist or Methodist. Moreover, First African Presbyterian Church comprised people who had many of the same aspirations as those who followed Richard Allen out of the White St. George's Methodist Church. They wanted a house of worship of their own, a preacher of their own color, and freedom from restrictions imposed by worshiping under the same roof with Whites who called them inferior.

John Gloucester, the pastor of First African, was as much a part of Black church leadership in Philadelphia as were Richard Allen and Absalom Jones, although Gloucester did not have the size following they had. But all of the Philadelphia, Baltimore, and New York clergy were relatively close in those days. They participated in the same uplifting and benevolent causes in behalf of both slaves and free Blacks. They worked together across denominational lines to lay a foundation for the African American culture and religion of their time. They were all pioneers of the Black church.

In theory, the presbyteries exercised the same jurisdiction over their African American churches as over their White congregations. In practice, however, African American congregations were usually free to do what they pleased in the Black world as long as they did not grossly disobey Presbyterian law. They did, nevertheless, experience many instances of discrimination. When David Laney, the father of Lucy Craft Laney, was ordained by Hopewell Presbytery, he was required to promise that he would restrict his preaching to African Americans only. He is reputed to have said afterward, "I'll preach to any damn body I please."

Even in the North, African American Presbyterians suffered indignities, were overlooked by their White counterparts, and were generally considered marginal to the mainstream of the denomination. It is not surprising, therefore, that even though they identified with an overwhelmingly White denomination and spurned efforts to encourage them to leave it, African American Presbyterian pastors and members were frequently gathering themselves in ethnic caucuses well before the end of the nineteenth century. The history of African Americans within the Presbyterian Church will clearly support the position that their congregations in the North and their separate judicatories in the South have always been a part of the larger Black church family. It is historical arrogance on the part of non-Presbyterian Blacks to regard us otherwise.

But what about the allegation that Black Presbyterians are on a higher socioeconomic plane than brothers and sisters in the Baptist, Methodist, and Pentecostal churches?

That may have been true at one time, but no longer. As much as some of us may prefer to think otherwise, African American Presbyterians are no island unto themselves. Taken as a whole, statistics show that mainstream African American churches have changed considerably over the past forty or fifty years and have caught up with us. In spite of appearances to the contrary, the Black church today is basically a middle-class institution. African American Presbyterian clergy will still show a slightly higher level of formal theological education than their counterparts in, say, Baptist, Holiness, and Pentecostal churches, but in terms of the annual income of their members, education, home ownership, value of church property, and individual tastes and aspirations, there is little if any difference between us and most other African American churches. In the steady growth of the American middle class since the Second World War, African American church people have enjoyed a sizable proportion of the general upward mobility of most Americans, and Black Presbyterian and Episcopal churches, which once boasted a preeminent class status, can do so no more.

The June/July 1981 issue of *Dollars and Sense* reported that more than twenty million Black churchgoers contributed $1.7 billion to their churches. In 1997 that figure is estimated to be closer to $3 billion. Fifteen years ago there were five million active African American church members in regular Sunday attendance who owned and operated 65,000 separate church properties worth $10.2 billion. All of those figures need to be upgraded today. In 1997 it is even more true than in 1981 that when the average African American minister preaches from Luke 4:18—"The Spirit of the Lord is upon me, because he has anointed me to bring good news to the poor"—people in the pews look around to see if any of "the poor" are present. When the preacher denounces crass, monopolistic capitalism in the United States, he or she may be offending members of the congregation. They are, after all, benefiting from capitalism, and more and more of them may have a negative response to the call for African American Christians to undertake ethical and political action to change the American economic system.

What we are saying has been true for some time of Presbyterian, African Methodist, and many Baptist churches, but today it is also more or less true of the Church of God in Christ, the Seventh-Day Adventists, and the Pentecostal Assemblies of the World. These denominations too, and others like them, increasingly exhibit the educational levels, individualism, and optimistic outlook that makes them middle class in any ordinary sense of the term.

As far as social status is concerned, the Presbyterians, Episcopalians, and the most fashionable Baptist and Methodist congregations may be a notch above these newer denominations, but in terms of self-image and cultural orientation, what were formerly regarded as backward, fundamentalist sects are full-fledged churches today. They are taking leadership in the community right alongside the older Black churches and, in some places around the country, even exceeding them in Christian education and social action.

Understanding Who African American Presbyterians Are Today

To say that mainstream African American churches, including Presbyterian, are basically middle class is not to say that there are no longer any poor people in them. That would be patently untrue. We are far from saying that our churches are so bourgeois that they should no longer be expected to attract the homeless and hungry, the people who live in the projects, and the millions who are keeping their noses just above the poverty line. What then are we trying to say by this discussion? Two points are being made that may sound contradictory but deserve careful consideration if we are to understand an ambivalent situation that continues to baffle some of our leaders.

First, Presbyterians have no special status that justifies the old pretension of exclusivity. We need to come down to earth and take our place with the rest of the African American church family.

Second, Black Presbyterians own for themselves and are connected to wealth and cannot avoid using the resources of a relatively privileged position to uplift their less privileged brothers and sisters.

As incredible as it may seem, some African American Presbyterians think of their church as a cut above more traditional Black churches. At the same time, they excuse themselves from active involvement in the ghetto by insisting that they themselves are needy and should be receiving help from their wealthy White church! They have, in other words, found a convenient but false reason for not giving more service to the much more desperate plight of their neighbors.

In order to understand African American Presbyterian congregations, our strengths and weaknesses, it is helpful to compare ourselves with historic Black congregations—such as those of the African Methodist Episcopal, the Christian Methodist Episcopal, the National Baptist Convention, Inc., or the Church of God in Christ—on some basis other than class. African American churches of the traditional Black denominations are different from us in three significant areas that deserve study: first, historical consciousness; second, self-image in relation to White people; and third (with subtle but notable changes in recent years), ethos, that is, the quality or texture of the worship and communal life of the congregation. Of course, there are conspicuous exceptions to these generalizations. The reader will have to judge whether or not his or her particular congregation fits the picture we are about to draw.

Historical Consciousness

Let's begin with how we regard our corporate past as a church. Although most Black Baptist and African Methodist churches are middle class in the sense we are using that term, they still have a feeling of continuity with and relationship to a more humble "Black past." To the early development of the National Baptist Convention, Inc., or the "Boyd Convention," if they are Baptist, or if Methodist, they will hark back to some of the great bishops and General Conferences of African Methodism. If they are Pentecostal, they will trace their origin to the great Azusa Street revival in the ghetto of Los Angeles.

Because these churches did not inherit their buildings from White congregations of the same denomination (as did many Presbyterian churches) or subsist for years on the largess of White mission funds, they have a recollection of a past that is "ethnically specific." By this we mean that their recollection of an earlier time does not include entangling relationships with White people. Of course, several Black denominations were formed by coming out of predominantly White churches, but most of their people have no institutional memory, generally speaking, of negotiations, visitations, accepting aid, using Sunday school material, or engaging in training and recreational programs in which White people played the dominant role.

These churches have been, for the most part, enclosed in a cocoon of Black history that may go back, like the Pentecostals for example, just to the early years of this century, but they are rooted in and conditioned by the enormous institutionalization of an African American denomination *qua African American.* They have, in other words, a Black national past in a different way than do we Presbyterians. They remember the heroes and heroines of that past and have been taught to be aware of the ties by which they are bound to them. Most African American Presbyterians, particularly in the North, where there were no all-Black judicatories, lack this kind of memory, except in a very local sense. They have, as a result, no consciousness of an existence that is part and parcel of the pilgrimage of African American people as a whole. Their memory is not separate, in any meaningful way, from the history of White people.

Self-Image in Relation to Whites

Second, it would seem to follow that the historic African American churches carry an image of themselves that grows out of an independent past rather than out of a past of being tethered to White Americans. The identity of the historic Black churches may not be as sharp as it should be, but it is usually not confused by the bipolarity that Du Bois called "double consciousness." What are we trying to say?

When one speaks of a "Black religious tradition" at the Wheat Street Baptist Church of Atlanta or the Mother Bethel AME Church of Philadelphia, the words have a ring of authenticity that needs no explanation. Indeed, an explanation may get a huffily raised eyebrow among people who never had any doubt that they were Black, that they were kith and kin of the African American community on the other side of the street, or that they participate from day to day in all the characteristics that come with the neighborhood, both positive and negative.

That is not ordinarily the case with African American Presbyterian churches. More often than not, there is a confused identity among us—a self-image that is, at best, incomplete, and at worst is inextricably mixed up with what we think Presbyterianism means to the White folks who brought this church with them from Scotland and Ireland and were good enough to let us share it with them.

Self-image is important for self-esteem and self-understanding. If you were to ask what a congregation should look like when it is both Black and Presbyterian, as we are doing in this book, most African American Presbyterians would find it difficult to respond, and some would even resent the question.

Ethos, or Quality of Worship and Communal Life

Finally, the ethos, or spiritual quality, of the historic African American churches is what we would call "that old-time religion" rather than the more sophisticated "new-time religion" of the mainline White denominations. This has been changing among many African American Presbyterian congregations during the past ten or twenty years; in any case, these comments are not to be taken as an endorsement for "the old-time religion," Black or White. But for most of our history, Black Presbyterian churches have worshiped and fellowshiped as our White brothers and sisters do. We have no sense of a distinctive Black ethos that we have shaped to fit our own brand of Presbyterianism.

The ambience of traditional African American churches is "down-home," rural, perfectionist, and evangelistic despite modernizing influences. There is a sort of African American twist or spin to all of those characteristics we have carried over from nineteenth-century Protestant evangelicalism that makes the ethos, or spiritual climate, of most Black churches feel like something different from suburban White Protestantism. One would not, for example, mistake the worship service and congregational life of an AME Zion congregation in upstate New York or Church of God in Christ congregation in Harlem for those of a White United Methodist church in Scarsdale, New York, or an American Baptist church in Hollywood, California. Whatever is meant by "that old-time religion" in both White and Black settings today—spirited preaching, extemporaneous prayer, sentimentally individualistic hymns, biblical literalism, unabashed and unchecked emotionalism, and an emphasis on the "family values" of Middle America—it is more normative for the historic Black churches than for African American Presbyterians. That special twist of the Black ethos is more likely to be present in the independent Black churches than in ours, although today we are trying it on for size.

One should hasten to say that in either case, much of the old lifestyle is gone. In traditional Black churches, certain secular adjustments are being made from Monday through Saturday in the "old-time religion." There is an increasing contradiction between what many Black congregations preach and what they practice. Nevertheless, both ministers and members seem blandly accommodated to the contradictions in a way that African American Presbyterians and Episcopalians are not. As one Pentecostal minister once said to me: "I don't believe in no seminary trainin' as necessary to preach. Seminary can even ruin the whoop of a Black preacher. But I sure would 'preciate some help with them seminary subjects you fellows teach up there."

Not only had he reconciled himself to the contradiction of wanting a theological education while disparaging it, he was even willing to take on what, in his case, would be the enormous task of qualifying for admission to the Colgate Rochester Divinity School in Rochester, New York. That proved to be impossible, so he began a special program for nonseminary ministers and approached the work with a mixture of pragmatism and a refreshing innocence that, when you really examined it, was without guile.

"Most of these courses," he slyly observed about the seminary curriculum, "are like eating fish. You have to swallow the meat and spit the bones out."

This attitude of an unschooled African American Pentecostal minister is not atypical. Many old-style Black preachers are gradually shifting out of a conservative ethos and are accepting the advantages of a more liberal theological education without feeling guilty about it. They already know who they are and what they have to do. There is little confusion about their basic identity as African American Christians who are immersed in the culture of the Black community but see the necessity of making adjustments to meet the paradoxes of the present age without completely disavowing the securities of the past.

In contrast, many African American Presbyterians either lack enough self-consciousness about what has happened to them to be as candid as the pastor in the special program at Colgate Rochester or are painfully disturbed by the tension they sense existing between a Black religious past and some vague notion about what it takes to be genuinely Presbyterian.

The Need for Clarity

Most of our people know that there ought to be some logical reason why they have chosen to remain Presbyterian rather than shift membership to a Black Baptist or Methodist church, but they are not sure what it is. They are not clear about what permits them to belong to a predominantly White church while simultaneously insisting on the right, if not the necessity, to affirm their need to identify with the African American religious tradition. They are eating the fish, bones and all.

We are not prepared at this point to make more of a value judgment about the difference between the two identities than we have thus far explored. More will be said about that later. The main point here is that there *are* differences, and some of them are important enough to induce what we would call an identity crisis among African American Presbyterians that many Baptists, Methodists, and Pentecostals never experience, unless they too venture outside of the familiar boundaries of the Black community.

It is the position of this author that such a crisis is healthy for intelligent African American Presbyterians, who want to get themselves together theologically and ecclesiastically; who want to sing the Lord's song in a strange land. But you have to know how the words and the music go if the purpose

Black and Presbyterian

is not only to get rid of a feeling of loneliness and estrangement from "the old folks at home" but to make a contribution to the rising chorus of those who would belong to the coming world church of the twenty-first century.

Questions for Discussion

Scripture for Reflection: James 5:19–20

1. Are African American Presbyterians more comfortable with European culture than with African Black culture? Would true evangelism in inner-city communities that resulted in increased membership of the underclass disturb the "Afro-Saxon" psyche?

2. What factors have contributed to many Christian churches becoming home to middle-class Blacks, while isolating or ignoring the needs of low-income Blacks?

3. Many Presbyterians and governing bodies in other denominations are encouraging the creation of multicultural church development. In most instances, racial ethnics, African Americans, and Africans in particular, have responded to this challenge by consciously deciding to attend predominantly White churches. However, a much smaller percentage of White people unite with predominantly African American congregations.

   ◆ Why have not more White people joined African American congregations?

   ◆ What has your presbytery or governing body done to encourage White people to affiliate with African American congregations? If there are not any noteworthy examples in your presbytery's history, what strategies would you recommend?

4. Can African American Presbyterians fully participate in denominational functions and still maintain a strong sense of involvement in African American communities?

   ◆ List other African American Presbyterian churches that have done this well.

   ◆ List the non-Presbyterian African American churches that have done this well.

5. Are African American Presbyterians schizophrenic? Support your answer.

6. In your opinion, is the Presbyterian Church a racist institution?

An *identity crisis* is an event in the development of a person or group when a decision must be made to either affirm or deny one's historical individuality.

6 Resolving an Identity Crisis

Although African American Presbyterians share many of the increasingly middle-class indicators of other Christians in the United States today, being members of the Presbyterian Church has partially cut us off from the religious culture of historic African American Christianity. Because of the detour that we Black Presbyterians have made, we stand in a more critical situation *vis-à-vis* the present cultural and theological revival and the renewed mission to the most needy sectors of the community to which some churches seem committed. Although we are beginning to change in preaching, music, liturgy, polity, patterns, and styles of congregational life, we are still not exactly Black nor exactly White. We are somewhere in between, and that makes some of us deeply uncomfortable. We are biting our fingernails.

We Presbyterians, in other words, have an identity crisis. We have become more and more aware that going to church is too often an unreflective, ineffective parenthesis between eleven and one o'clock on Sundays and the rest of the week. Because many of us continue to be sincere and well-meaning people, that bothers us. We sense that the Black cultural experience in which we and our families participate during most of the week is segmental and marginal rather than integral to our faith and woven into the whole fabric of our existence. The result is that some of us who want to be well-grounded theologically in a faith that we are living out everyday in fact feel guilty about our shallowness and our hypocrisy.

So we are at a critical juncture in African American Presbyterian history. What makes it critical is that when we are asked the important theological question "What does it really mean to be Black and Presbyterian?" most of us are either silent or confused. This question is not as new as it may sound, for some of our people asked it in the Afro-American Presbyterian Council at the beginning of this century. Today, however, it is more important than ever, and, unlike a previous generation that more readily found its model in the White church, most of us today have no answer.

Some Presbyterians have a problem with identity without even knowing it. Fortunately (from one point of view), they are anesthetized against a crisis by an indifferent and conventional attitude about their faith. More unfortunate are those who are trying to make the Christian walk "with eyes wide open" and have begun to feel the pain of a double identity. We want to know how to stop the suffering. But that is an indication that we may be entering into the first stages of an identity crisis. We are beginning to make progress when we realize that such a crisis is necessary in order for some African American Presbyterians to find themselves and begin to make a contribution not only to the Black church but to the whole church of Christ. This contribution is one that others, because of the ironies of their denominational histories, may not be as well disposed or equipped to perform as we are. But before considering that possibility, we must deal with the key question of this chapter: What is an identity crisis?

An *identity crisis* is an event in the development of a person or group when a decision must be made to either affirm or deny one's historical individuality. By historical individuality we mean that putative uniqueness or distinctiveness that belongs to someone who is intensely aware of standing in a particular place, at a particular time, under a particular set of circumstances, all of which go into making that person or group who he, she, or it is. Racial and cultural groups, as well as persons, have an identity given from many different sources, such as genetic, sociological, historical, and political factors. When a person or a group asks, "Who am I?" or "Who are we?" a crisis of identity may have already begun in which some kind of decision needs to be made in order to resolve the tension, clear the air, get one's self out of an existential dilemma.

Often there is some external, foundation-shaking event that precipitates such a crisis. In any case, when a question of identity is resolved in terms that entail a rejection of an identity that was previously imposed on one by another person or group, we can be sure that there will be a crisis on both sides. Each must redefine self in relation to the other. This is, some psychologists say, a healthy state of affairs that may be the first step toward authentic reconciliation.

Every parent knows that not until a child expresses his or her historical individuality, becomes a person in his or her own right, is it possible to enjoy a mutually fulfilling relationship—a true, unequivocal community. That does not, however, happen when the child is still immature. When your infant refuses to take a bottle or unceremoniously shoves a plate of strained fruit off the table, you suddenly realize that you have an individual human being on your hands. Frustrations, disappointments, problems? Yes, for everyone concerned. But in those days of infancy, there was not much of a crisis after all. A small tantrum did not have to be taken too seriously. The real identity crisis comes later when you can no longer use a piece of candy, a lecture, or the keys to the family car to control another's behavior. It is when a full-grown adult person stands up to you, eyeball to eyeball, and tells you off, that you have an identity crisis on your hands.

The Special Responsibility of Presbyterians

A crisis of identity is not unique to African American Presbyterians, but its resolution opens up an area of special responsibility for us. Many of us who lived through the 1960s and understood what was going on (for example, in the rise of Black Power or the creation of Black Presbyterians United) experienced such a crisis, although we may not have seized the responsibilities that went with it. By now some of us have slipped back into a previous condition of cultural anomie and "Whitenization" without even knowing it. For us, the 1960s need to happen all over again. Others of us have consciously and deliberately resisted the vocational implications of the crisis and have fallen back into a safe and painless accommodation to the color blindness and ethnic neutrality that is a game White Presbyterians sometimes play. Today, they are doubtful that there is any continuing meaning and purpose of the African American experience in the melting pot of this reunited Presbyterian Church (U.S.A.).

The position of this book is that serious Christians of color, wherever they live in the world and whatever their denomination may be, cannot take the matter of cultural and ethnic identity lightly. We have to make some kind of decision. The issue for the sector of the one, holy, catholic, and apostolic church that happens to be African American is this: How can we use the history, culture, and present experience of our struggle for full humanity, freedom, and equality to enhance the proclamation of the gospel of Jesus Christ and the demonstration of Christ's power to transform not only African American persons but also the whole human race?

That may seem like a tall order for any group of African American Christians, and particularly for a tiny minority of Black men and women within this particular denomination. But we remember the word of the Lord to Jeremiah when God commanded him to buy a field in an apparently doomed land: "Is anything too hard for me?" (Jer. 32:27).

It well may be that those who have experienced the curious dilemma of being, at one time or another, on both sides of the color line in churches such as the Presbyterian, have special resources and responsibilities not available to most members of the historic Black churches, despite the advantages they enjoy that we explored in the previous chapter. But the most effective utilization of those resources plus the faithful discharge of the responsibilities afforded us by our historic relationship to White Presbyterians await the resolution of our crisis of identity. We need to discover, or rediscover, what Queen Esther found out— that God does not want us to abandon our own people when they need us most, and that we African American Presbyterians may indeed have "come to royal dignity for just such a time as this" (Esth. 4:14). We are, of course, free to take a pill and forget the whole thing.

A Black Christian View of Our "Twoness"

W.E.B. Du Bois wrote about the situation in which many thoughtful people find themselves. The quotation that follows has been analyzed *ad nauseam*, but still helps to clarify our basic dilemma. We have seen how, in his masterful *The Souls of Black Folk*, Du Bois spoke of African Americans having "two souls, two thoughts, two unreconciled strivings; two warring ideals in one dark body, whose dogged strength alone keeps it from being torn asunder."[1]

Many of us are conscious of this "twoness," particularly in the sense that a considerable part of our life, qualitatively if not quantitatively, has been moving back and forth between the two worlds of Black and White in America. The twoness, the double consciousness, the ambivalence is the cause of the identity crisis we continue to experience. But the paradox is that although it defines the nature of an intrinsic weakness, it also, as Du Bois suggests, includes the "dogged strength" that keeps us "from being torn asunder." This striking way of putting the dilemma catches the physical as well as the psychological causes and manifestations of this condition of twoness.

But from a Black Christian perspective, Du Bois did not go far enough. The twoness itself can be a source of strength, not because of some reservoir of inner power and nobility we possess as a race, but because of the unmerited grace of God through the sacrifice of God's incarnate and crucified one, Jesus Christ. Du Bois, perhaps, was not enough of a Christian to go that far, but African American Presbyterians—indeed, Black Christians as a whole—can go that far. We can affirm that the strength of the African American people, combining the best and worst of two cultures, comes from God who gives to all daughters and sons the grace and power to transcend the contradictions and delusions of our human experience. Moreover, we believe that "dogged strength" confers a special responsibility and evokes a special religious faith at this time in history.

We emphasize *religious* faith because the reigning ideals of secularism, no matter how enlightened, lack the emotional depth and compelling motivation necessary to grasp the totality of our being and turn us toward the forgiveness and love of God without which it is not possible to experience true humanity. And what is true for the person is also true, in this instance, for the group. The alienation and hatred that divides and sickens the world cannot be overcome by secular ideologies but only by faith in Christ. Being like ourselves except for sin, Christ has taken us into himself and "has broken down the dividing wall" between African Americans and those who despise and oppress us, so that he "might reconcile both groups to God in one body through the cross, thus putting to death that hostility through it" (Eph. 2:14, 16).

Thus the Christian faith provides African American culture and religion with a spiritual cement by which two cultures, one African by origin and the other Euro-American by assimilation and adoption, are reinterpreted and fused into one new creation. This new creation is a new African American existence and identity that has the power to inspire and direct Black people in the United States toward the goal of shalom, the Hebraic idea of the welfare, peace, and unity of the whole created order.

The problem of the African American church, as the principal carrier of this—according to Du Bois—"gift of Black folk," is that one part of it has retained Blackness without the sense of a cultural vocation, while the other part is tempted to give up Black culture in the interest of what it perceives as a calling to a wider, more universal fellowship. That division does not frustrate African American Presbyterians only. It runs through all our predominantly Black churches.

In both cases, the power of the African American religious experience to clarify certain foundational aspects of the human condition and inspire people to transcend the contradictions of existence is waived or remains underutilized. It is precisely through its "twoness"—through the synthesis of its two historic components without obliterating either—that African American religious faith has its greatest value for these times. But faith in God is the essential factor. Take away faith in God's action in history and both aspects of what we call African American culture collapse. Take away equal emphasis on Blackness and its vocation not only to liberate African Americans but also to reconcile all who are estranged from brothers and sisters, and the religious experience of our slave forebears is falsified and betrayed.

Black theology, which made its debut in American intellectual circles in the late 1960s, is an attempt to hold all of this together in a plausible theory and praxis predicated on the revelation of God in Jesus Christ, the Liberator and Reconciler. It is the ongoing process of reflecting on and ordering the substance of African American religion and culture in the United States in such a way as to evaluate them both in the critical light of, and in coherence with, the gospel of Christ. The consequence of such theological reflection and praxis will be the liberation of us all, White, Black, and otherwise, from racism, poverty, and oppression. But it also means the end of innocence. It means courageously facing and resolving the crisis of identity that has come to the breaking point for African Americans in this twentieth century of the Christian movement.

In prospect is a new creation. The old enmities and alienation have already been overcome by the sacrificial gift of Jesus Christ—as the apostle Paul reminds us—"through the blood of his cross" (Col. 1:20). Is it possible, we ask, that we will all witness this new creation and that Black Presbyterians, because of the particularity of their experience in this predominantly White church, have a distinctive role to play? The answer is, we believe, affirmative. That is, indeed, the essential message of this book. We turn in chapter 7 to examine some of the ways, or strategies, by which this special role and responsibility may be discharged today.

Questions for Discussion

Scripture for Reflection: James 3:13–18

1. Reflect on your purpose in the Presbyterian Church. Does your involvement in this denomination in some way benefit the African American community? If yes, explain. If no, list three ways that you might be able to do so.

2. How might Black theology help African American Presbyterians find their identity? What is Black theology?

3. As an African American Presbyterian, are you one who has chosen to retain your Blackness, or have you chosen assimilation for more universal fellowship? Explain.

   ◆ Does your pastor integrate the teaching of Black theology?

4. What were your strongest emotions as you read this chapter? Explain.

5. What does it mean to you to be Black and Presbyterian?

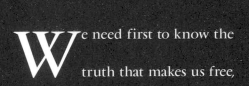

We need first to know the truth that makes us free, which is the essence of theology.

7

Resources of the African American Christian Tradition

The situation in which many African American Presbyterians find themselves can be described as an identity crisis. We are, of course, not the only Christians who are asking questions about ethnic identity and role. Today, African American scholars in religion have produced excellent resources that can help all of us decide who we are and what God wants us to do. It is not ethnic chauvinism for some of us who are members of the Presbyterian Church (U.S.A.) to lay claim to these resources that are, not withstanding our past disinterest, as accessible to us as they are to the historic Black denominations.

We Black Presbyterians are no less intelligent than other Christians. We believe in serving the same God with our whole heart, mind, and strength. We are sincere in our loyalty to the church in which we were baptized or to which, for one reason or another, we have transferred our membership. Many of us take seriously the fact that we are in a church that professes multiculturalism and, in recent years, has taken some pains to ensure that we and other minorities are proportionately represented at most levels of the church's life. That does not always come off as planned and, from our point of view, is not even always necessary, for some days we feel like being integrated and some days we don't. Yet we know that at least fairness was intended and written into the laws that governed the reunion of the Presbyterian Church U.S. and the United Presbyterian Church U.S.A. in 1983.

But when we stop to think about our role in this denomination, when the church asks us to put up or shut up, to make our unique contribution as a minority group that has come of age in this particular church, we are often reduced to silence or we flounder in embarrassing confusion. Some of our White friends and allies are equally confused because the most sensitive among them hope that we have not been swallowed up and still have a history and culture that can enrich their lives as well as ours. But most of our friends would say that they don't pretend to have the competence to spell out for us the meaning of that history and culture or the role we should play. They would admit that although the meaning of the Reformed tradition for Whites in the contemporary Presbyterian Church has been spelled out, no one has bothered to do the same for Blacks.

The maturity that we want to celebrate demands that we stand on our own feet. For the past thirty years our seminaries have been turning out African American Presbyterian ministers whom we might have expected to define our mission and ministry and lead us to a useful appropriation of the history and meaning of the Black presence within this predominantly White church. The time has come, however, when we must confess that, on the whole, they have not produced that kind of leadership for our churches. Whether the fault is in the theological seminaries or in the congregations that have called but refused to permit their pastors to lead them intellectually, or have failed to demand more from them is beside the point at the moment. The point we are making now is that African American Presbyterians have a problem fully participating in this church as a people who use the resources of an inheritance that antedates American slavery, one we share with other African and African American Christians.

Let us consider the reasons for our identity crisis.

Diagnosing an Identity Crisis

Insufficient Knowledge of Black History

First, most of us have insufficient information about the history of God's dealings with the ancient people of Africa, or of Christianity in Africa in the early centuries of the church, or even of our own involvement, as African Americans, in American Presbyterianism. And there is no excuse for it. A considerable body of literature now exists on African traditional religions and African insights into the mystery of God's encounter with humankind; on Black people in the biblical world; on the significance of Egypt, Ethiopia, and Nubia in the first millennium of Christian history; on Black Christianity and other religions that were influenced by African retentions in the New World. Also, there is a growing body of material on African Americans in the Presbyterian churches. The information we need is available; we need only to consult it.

At the Interdenominational Theological Center (ITC) in Atlanta, of which Johnson C. Smith Presbyterian Seminary is a participating institution, African American scholarship that researches, teaches, and writes about these subject areas has been going on for many years. The trailblazing work of Professor Charles B. Copher, the preeminent African American scholar in biblical and theological issues bearing on the Black religious experience, was carried on at the ITC until his retirement in 1978. Other younger African American teachers and writers, such as Cain Hope Felder, Randall Bailey, Clarice Martin, Renita Weems, Thomas Hoyt, and many others have contributed to a growing body of knowledge that helps us understand the meaning and significance of the word *African* in the term *African American Christianity.*

Few of us have bothered to delve into this material, and some of our pastors, who have studied at universities and seminaries where such subject matter may have been taught, have not learned how to apply it in their ministries. At presbytery meetings or meetings at the denominational offices in Louisville, one still runs into African American laity who have been effectively brainwashed to ignore or disparage this inheritance. Some of them have never heard that such resources exist. Others may be aware that the Presbyterian Church claims to be antiracist and has done certain things to encourage African American participation. But they have not thought about nor been advised about the role that Blacks have played in the history of Christianity in Africa or twentieth-century American religious history. They have no idea of how or why we have shaped and been shaped by a long association with White Presbyterians in the United States.

This informational vacuum should come as no surprise. With exceptions that can be counted on the fingers of one hand, none of the scores of books and journal articles available on the favorite topics of Presbyterians—Calvin in Geneva; Knox's struggle with Mary, Queen of Scots; the development of the church in colonial America; doctrinal controversies surrounding the Westminster Confession; Presbyterian roles in the Great Awakenings; denominational schisms; ecclesiastical restructuring; and the ecumenical movement—none of these touch on the kind of scholarship to which African Americans have been contributing over the past thirty years. With the exception of our beloved Johnson C. Smith Seminary at the ITC, Presbyterian seminaries scarcely know such scholarship exists, and if they know, they don't care.

The work of Black biblical scholars on the presence of Africa in biblical literature aside, what are White Presbyterian professors telling their students who African and African American Christians are today, what we have contributed to the church in the past, and how our role and mission should be understood in the contemporary church? There is no wonder that our seminarians and lay people are ill-equipped to deal with the question "What does it mean to be Black and Christian?" much less "What does it mean to be Black and Presbyterian?"

Ignorance of Black Theology

Second, there is no appreciation of what happened in American theology since the Civil Rights movement and the emergence of Black theology. Of particular importance to us, for example, are the writings and organizing work of those who created the Black theology movement in the United States and overseas: James H. Cone, Cecil Cone, J. Deotis Roberts, Albert Pero, Joseph Washington, Olivia Pearl Stokes, William Eichelberger, C. Eric Lincoln, Shawn Copeland, Allan Boesak, Desmond Tutu, Ambrose Moyo, to name a few.

A veritable revolution broke out among African American scholars, ministers, and church executives after the founding of the National Committee of Black Churchmen (later to become the National Committee of Black Christians) in 1967. The publication of James H. Cone's *Black Theology and Black Power* in 1969 helped to usher in this Black consciousness in religion that had an impact on both American Protestantism and Roman Catholicism that was out of all proportion to the number of people who participated in the fledgling movement. But little or none of this has been passed down to the people in the pews. Our church, which emphasizes the importance of Christian education for the cultivation of an intelligent and well-informed laity, has rarely encouraged Sunday schools in African American churches to study the activity of God in the Black experience and how reflection on that experience can help to make the faith more true and exciting for our children.

Here again, it is not altogether clear where we ought to lay the blame. Has the denomination failed us in this regard, or have we pastors and leaders inoculated our people against Christian education keyed to a Black theological perspective? Perhaps the denomination and our own people have to share the blame equally, but the result is the same. We Black Presbyterians are ignorant of African American theological reflection from slavery to the Black consciousness movement of the twentieth century. As a result, some who have struggled in the name of Christ for freedom and justice in both the church and American society are not able to enter an intellectually credible plea "to make [our] defense to anyone who demands . . . an accounting for the hope that is in [us]" (1 Peter 3:15).

That is regrettable, for if the struggle against slavery, racial segregation and discrimination, and in behalf of human and civil rights has ultimate meaning for African Americans, then Black theology is an authentic method of reflecting on and speaking about God in our experience, and most of us who are believers should be able to profess our faith in Christ in those terms without embarrassment.

Neglect of Organization

Third, there is a lack of participation of both clergy and laity in the National Black Presbyterian Caucus, the instrument African American Presbyterians have employed, under various names, for addressing the issues in the Presbyterian Church that concerned them since before the Civil War. What we formerly called Black Presbyterians United (BPU) became in 1983 the National Black Presbyterian Caucus (NBPC)—"a nonprofit organization whose main purpose is to affirm an authentic African American religious witness; to enhance the witness and ministry of Presbyterian churches serving in predominantly African American communities; and to be a conscience of the Presbyterian Church in promoting racial justice and eliminating racial oppression."[1]

The phenomenon of denominational ethnic caucuses is well known in the United States. During the Civil Rights movement, the various African American caucuses diverted mainstream Protestantism and Roman Catholicism from a wait-and-see, conservative attitude regarding the struggle for racial justice to active participation in the movement that was founded by Dr. Martin Luther King Jr. The success of the African American caucuses in getting the predominantly White churches and the National Council of the Churches of Christ to recognize the urgency of racial justice inspired the organization of similar caucuses among Native, Hispanic, and Asian Americans. These four caucus groups within the Presbyterian family now meet together periodically to support their individual and common goals and promote the spirit of multiculturalism in the denomination as a whole.

But caucuses have a way of coming together in emergencies and falling apart when the emergencies are over. The National Black Presbyterian Caucus has always been more impressive during crises and on the national scene rather than in the day-to-day work required locally and regionally. Also, there is a difference between a political caucus that comes together for serious study, strategy development, and collaboration on policies and programs affecting the life of the church in the African American community, and what might be called "social caucusing." The latter has to do primarily with the fun and fellowship that is diluted in interracial or multicultural settings. Social caucusing may indeed be necessary during this period of uncertainty about Black identity, but it has not served well to cultivate a theologically astute and mission-oriented clergy and laity.

The watchdog function of a political caucus requires constant vigilance at presbytery by a well-trained laity interested in developing African American Presbyterianism in faith and order, evangelism, and social mission. Any ethnic minority that is, as we are, less than 5 percent of a large, bureaucratic denomination like the Presbyterian Church (U.S.A.) is bound to be practically invisible without a caucus. Individuals and congregations need the support and counsel of a citywide or regional expression of some solidarity-promoting group that can assist them in making choices, setting goals, and finding their ecclesiastical bearings. It is too easy to be isolated and marginalized. The fact that most African American Presbyterians are not consistently involved in a presbytery-wide unit of the NBPC means that we are bereft of any meaningful unity. That lack is an important element of the problem of participating in the Presbyterian Church with power and a sense of responsibility for both its welfare and our own.

The question frequently arises, "Is an ethnic caucus really necessary today?" More than a casual study of the Presbyterian Church (U.S.A.) will reveal that racism still exists and is expressed in the attitudes, opinions, and actions of many Presbyterians whose lives intersect with Black lives every day except Sunday. It is institutionalized in decisions about how many and what African Americans should occupy key policy-making positions, in what topics have access to the agenda of presbytery councils and what is pushed under the table, in the services the church renders to itself and to the society.

Few Presbyterians think about how covert racism operates, for example, in a camp and conference program, a home for retired church workers, a church college or seminary, or in the denominational offices. The significance of NBPC is that it tries to monitor these and other sensitive areas. Intelligent, alert lay men and women are needed for this systematic monitoring. They help to keep our congregations aware of what is going on and whether or not the church is living up to its commitments to racial justice, pluralism, and equal opportunity. The caucus reminds us of the resources of the African American Christian tradition. These resources give us a national posture and a local praxis for our discipleship in the still neglected African American community. They also pump us up with greater confidence in working alongside others for a more faithful and effective church.

Five Resources of the Tradition

If African American Presbyterians have anything of importance to bring to the Christian family, it is the resource of faith that has been shaped by our long pilgrimage from Africa to America. Without this faith, without the witness of men and women who understand and embrace such a resource, the American churches will be the poorer. Black Presbyterians need to lay claim to and share with others the following resources that are basic to the African American religious tradition.

Personal and Group Freedom

Freedom from White control is the keystone of the African American religious edifice. It was the reason for the preacher-led slave revolts, the "invisible institution" that gathered for worship under brush arbors of southern plantations, the schism led by Richard Allen and the African Methodists, and the emptying of the Southern Methodist, Baptist, and Presbyterian churches after the Civil War. At every point in the history of African American churches in this country is the desire for liberty, for bringing an end to White tutelage and paternalism.

The drive toward personal and group freedom is grounded in both the humanity of African American people and our intense appreciation of John 8:36: "So if the Son makes you free, you will be free indeed." Although that text may be interpreted in several ways, it has always pointed Black believers toward independence and self-reliance based on freedom through Jesus Christ. That sentiment is expressed in the struggle to throw off the shackles of slavery to find time and space within which we could worship in our own way, exercising the freedom of body and soul, and mobilizing and organizing ourselves through the church. Without the emphasis on freedom, the African American religious tradition is bereft of an anchor in Christ, for he has always been recognized as our Liberator par excellence. Because of the freedom our ancestors found in Christ, they came together in the only organization they were permitted to have, and the African American church was called into existence even before a regular family structure was legitimized.

The Image of Africa as the Land of Origin

The significance of the image of Africa as the land of origin is not so much that it is primarily about beginnings, but because it retains Africa as the place where the natural dispositions and gestures of Black people are confirmed and valorized. Historically, the African American church has thought of itself as an African rather than a "colored" or "Negro" institution. The one notable exception was the Colored Methodist Episcopal Church, which changed its name to the Christian Methodist Episcopal (CME) Church in 1954. In the earliest period, however, we had the *African* Baptists in Savannah, the *African* Methodists in Baltimore and New York, and the *African* Presbyterians in Philadelphia.

We can exaggerate the importance of this early connection with Africa, but it is true that authentic African American religion still retains a mystique around the image and symbolism of the continent of our origin. This is true, in spite of the fact that relatively few African Americans know much about Africa or desire to live there.

The mystique is both emotional and intellectual. It includes a recognition of God's primal dealings with Africa in the Old and New Testaments, and the expectation, as Ps. 68:31 was interpreted by previous generations of Black preachers, that Africa will someday be vindicated for her humiliation and despoilment and attain the greatness of her ancient past.

Many of the sermons and writings of African American preachers in the nineteenth century repeated these themes over and over. Benevolent societies and fraternal orders emphasized and ritualized the image of Africa—the one place in the world where the culture and spirit of the Black race could be freely expressed and esteemed. Black colleges and universities taught African history when it was practically unknown in White institutions of higher education. Our schools also took pains to bring African young men and women to the United States to receive their training and return home to help their people.

The first missionary outreach of African Americans was to the African continent. The "redemption of Africa" was the rallying cry throughout the nineteenth century. Many leaders, such as Bishop Henry M. Turner of the AME Church and Rev. Alexander Crummell of the Episcopal Church, believed that it was God's will for African Americans to return to the land of their ancestors.

The continent has not occupied the place in our religion and culture in the twentieth century that it enjoyed previously, but anyone who takes the trouble to investigate where the troops come from for Pan-Africanist causes in the United States will find that most of them are supplied by the churches. The religious concern for solidarity between Africa and the Diaspora has enormous implications. Behind the movement for Black consciousness and solidarity is the assumption that God did not leave our non-Christian ancestors without a witness. The image of Africa may be somewhat less prominent today than it was during the 1960s and 1970s, but it is still part of the tradition.

The Will of God for Social Justice

A third powerful resource of the African American Christian tradition is the widely held conviction in most of our churches that it is the will and purpose of God to establish justice in the earth—that justice making and peace making are of the highest priority to God and, therefore, should be to us. We have always believed that God wants the church to engage in the struggle for justice and human rights and that the engagement is an essential part of what it means to be a born-again Christian. That belief goes back to the first churches that supported the abolitionists and helped to create the Underground Railroad. There was the expectation that all African American clergy had to be "race men." Leaders were to use the political and economic power of their churches to defend the widow and the orphan, "to loose the bonds of injustice, to undo the thongs of the yoke, to let the oppressed go free, and to break every yoke" (Isa. 58:6).

The notion that religion and politics do not mix has always been contrary to this tradition. The old Black preachers knew their Old Testament. What impressed them was how "Daniel's God" acted in the affairs of the people. The Negro spirituals recall the exploits of the "Great God from Zion" and the intervention of "King Jesus" in behalf of those who are despised and abused in this world. As much as contemporary African American churches may attempt to underplay this emphasis, it continues to flex its muscles in times of resurgent racism, poverty, and unemployment, to force our preachers to return to the political arena or suffer the ridicule and contempt of the masses.

The influence of clergypersons such as Adam Clayton Powell, Jr., Martin Luther King Jr., John Hurst Adams, and Jesse Jackson may decline as some of their people join the ranks of the oppressors and show up at stadium rallies and television programs on the side of the Christian Right. But, the political salience of Black religion is tenacious. The radical tradition runs deep in the ghetto and the African American church continues to be motivated and energized by the exuberant politico-religiosity of the folk.

Creative Style and Artistry

Much has been written about this characteristic of Black culture, but there has been relatively little investigation of style and artistry as a continuing resource of the African American religious tradition. It is not easy to describe what we mean by style and artistry in religion. Anyone who has observed the tenor and tone of the preaching, prayers and testimonies, music, and general behavioral flamboyance of a traditional African American worship service on a Sunday morning has probably been struck by its spectacular quality.

Black worship is a theater of the divine. There is enormous performatory power in what on the surface may appear to be shoddy and disorderly but in fact is an intentionally crafted and stylized pattern of pastoral leadership and congregational response. The soul of the African American liturgy is seldom reflected in the printed order of service. In worship the people find elements that are exciting, spontaneous, and entertaining as well as edifying. In the aesthetic of this folk tradition, the "beauty of holiness" is not restricted to the consecratedness of the ritual or the people's contemplation of the divine perfections enthroned, as in the majesty of the Sistine Chapel.

This Black aesthetic involves an appreciation of human ability or panache in the execution of the praise of God, so that what takes place in the sanctuary makes God more palpable, more real. It not only invokes God but enfleshes God with finesse and artistry. The event of worship becomes satisfying to behold and participate in. African Americans ordinarily come out of church saying how much they "enjoyed" the service. They emerge into the strains and stresses of the outside world having participated in something special—the drama of salvation. The eloquent preacher, the robed, swinging choirs, the colorful congregation become the *dramatis personae* who have a flair about "processing" and "call and response," smoothly coordinating roles as they enter together into a symbolic enactment of "the story"—the message that has nourished the community through thick and thin. Although the congregation may be diverse in color, education, and class, this dramatic enactment of God's presence gives it a common identity through an empathetic bonding, or what Ralph Ellison has called "a concert of sympathies."

Creative style and artistry are cultural artifacts. They are part of the essence of African American ethnicity. They are rooted in the African inheritance. In a broader context, creative style and artistry are found in the orality, language, music, dress, cuisine, and the general *savoir faire* of the community. It is expressed specifically in the religious experience in terms of innovativeness in biblical interpretation and preaching, improvisation in hymnody, spontaneity in worship, and in the most sophisticated urban churches a subtle balance between emotional and intellectual content. Black Presbyterian churches sometimes lack these qualities because they have chosen to emulate White middle-class religion, but this is rapidly changing. Today more African American Presbyterians are discovering the aesthetic of the Black religious tradition.

The Unity of Secular and Sacred

In this last resource of the tradition we are dealing with the substructure on which all the others rest. Most scholars agree that the erasure of the line between the secular and the sacred, the profane and the holy, everyday life and fervid religiosity is an enduring feature of African religions. Many would go further and say that it is probably the most significant part of those religions that the African slaves brought to the New World. The worldview based on the unity of the secular and the sacred is a peculiarity of all African and African-descended societies that have not been totally acculturated by the fallout of the eighteenth-century Enlightenment and the scientific revolution. The habit of dividing reality into two parts and consigning the smaller sector to "things religious" seems endemic to Euro-American civilizations. However, this sharp dichotomy between religion and the rest of life was unknown in Africa until quite recently. Although it was greatly blunted before 1750 in North America, the unified, or holistic, perspective continued to embody the folk tradition for the next two hundred years.

This, of course, does not mean that the folk tradition did not recognize the difference between "praying and ploughing" or that they lived in a totally divinized world that rejected any intrusion of reason and the scientific method. The question here is whether or not, as religious beliefs developed under modernity, the baby was thrown out with the bath water. Black Christianity with its African background may have been more successful than its White counterpart in finding an acceptable accommodation between the worldview of the Bible and that of modern science.

When we spoke earlier about "pragmatic spirituality" in the African American church, we were trying to describe the religious worldliness that does not hesitate to use the church as much for winning strikes and elections as saving souls. There may be a better way of putting it, but pragmatic spirituality suggests a different orientation than spirituality based on the absolute polarity of the holy and worldly aspects of life.

Nevertheless, Black religion and folklore have shown a persistent tolerance for the mysterious and occult. Many of us still believe that the spiritual is pervasive in the world—that behind the world we see and handle is another, invisible world that is no less real and efficacious for good or ill. Such a view may be old-fashioned, but it coheres well with Scripture. The miraculous power of Jesus and his disciples is taken for granted. The inauguration of this One from Galilee meant that God changed things—"rescued us from . . . darkness and transferred us into the kingdom of his beloved Son" (Col. 1:13). African Americans for whom the church is indispensable believe that we already exist in a new creation where God is not under obligation to the laws that science has thus far learned, with many more to be discovered. This does not mean that we are antiscientific, but that the God we serve is free to work in the interest of the forgiveness of sin on earth and cosmic redemption in the worlds that lie beyond.

Religion, from this perspective, has to do with all of life, and all of life has to do with religion. The same beat that stirs our souls when "the good times roll" on a Saturday night satisfies them in another context on Sunday morning. Aretha Franklin learned how to sing the blues by singing gospel. Martin Luther King Jr. marched thousands to the picket line with the same music and the same spirit with which he marched them down the aisles of churches in Selma, Alabama, or Washington, D.C.

To say that we are "a religious people"[2] is not to pretend that we are still living in a precognitive world relying on magic and charms while others depend on reason and technology. It simply means that we do not believe that God is dead. It is incumbent on us, therefore, to find appropriate ways to serve a living God. Through suffering and struggle we have learned how to praise God while marching to war as Christian soldiers. We are, at one and the same time, a religious people who are not afraid to look bitter reality in the face and a secular people who have heard and believed the gospel of redemption.

Preserving the Values of Black Faith

These, then, are the primary resources of the tradition that have always been accessible to us. We have only had to reach into the history and culture of our people to claim them. Not enough has been written about the continuing vitality of this kind of religion in the African American community. Whether it will enrich the life of the new middle class in the future depends in large measure on how much our churches are willing and prepared to invest in it as a cultural vocation. Many church members need reorientation to this understanding of the tradition if it is to be preserved rather than permitted to fade into oblivion.

We have no need to canonize these resources and deny that there is any other way to apprehend the truth about nature, humanity, and God. We believe in progressive revelation—the gradual unfolding of truth as persons and groups dialogue around the issues that concern them. African Americans do not come to such a dialogue empty-headed. The long experience of becoming a people—of testing and experimentation, struggle and sacrifice on the way to the Promised Land—has deposited a wealth of knowledge and folk wisdom in the stream of our culture. We dare not ignore this or treat it lightly. Although Black-on-Black crime and individualism have taken their toll, one of the gifts of Black folk is that they understand the importance of peoplehood. We need to be encouraged not simply to hold on to this value and other values from the past but to build on them for the future. American culture and society as a whole will benefit from a revitalization of these traditional resources of the community.

On the basis of the meaning of the African American presence in Christianity as a whole, Black Presbyterians need to make a choice about whether we will enhance and further develop these resources or whether we will abandon them to the dusty bins of history. This drifting indifference with which too many Black Christians take church membership is unworthy of the One we profess to serve.

The options are open. We need first to know the truth that makes us free, which is the essence of theology. Then we need to make up our minds about our personal and collective vocations within this denomination. Will we try to serve Christ and the Presbyterian Church (U.S.A.) out of the African American religious heritage that has been passed down to us? Or will each of us melt into the woodwork and become just another brainwashed, middle-class "Oreo-Presbyterian"? Another option that some of our leaders are suggesting is that we come out of the Presbyterian Church (U.S.A.) altogether and form a new African American denomination of our own.

This may sound harsh and may be viewed as an attempt to stuff a painfully difficult decision down people's throats. But discipleship is serious business. Each of us has the right to have his or her personal decision respected—whatever it turns out to be. But we must decide!

Joshua said to the tribes of Israel at Shechem, "Choose this day whom you will serve" (Josh. 24:15). If we and our fellow church members really have no basis for making such a decision, that will be (alas!) all the worse for us and to the shame of our casual way of introducing people to the church without nurturing them after they become members.

We move now to ask what a decision to serve the Lord as African American Christians will look like within the Presbyterian Church (U.S.A.). The National Black Presbyterian Caucus and Johnson C. Smith Theological Seminary have addressed this question for several years in annual convocations and theological consultations. In the next chapter we will build on those discussions by exploring a new way of being an African American Presbyterian layperson or minister that takes into account all that we have been saying about the African American religious tradition.

Questions for Discussion

Scripture for Reflection: James 1:5–11

1. How familiar are you with materials and resources on God's dealings with the ancient people of Africa or African American Presbyterian history?

2. Does your congregation make a deliberate effort to teach the Bible from an African perspective—to celebrate African heritage through visuals, materials, and resources—or are only European images on the church's walls and the covers of resource materials?

3. Do conversations or topics pertaining to African American issues or problems make you uncomfortable in the presence of your European brothers and sisters?

4. Has the National Black Presbyterian Caucus been effective in accomplishing its goals of promoting racial justice and eliminating racial oppression? Is there still a need for a Black Caucus?

5. At one time in church history, all African American clergy were expected to use the political and economic power of their churches for improvement of the race. What in your opinion is expected of African American Presbyterian clergy today?

We need something that communicates what we value and disvalue in life; what we think about ourselves; how we view the world in the light of the gospel filtered through African American Christian sensibilities.

8

Toward a New Style of African American Presbyterianism

Dr. James H. Costen, retiring president of the Interdenominational Theological Center in Atlanta and former moderator of the 194th General Assembly, made a study of the African American constituency of the United Presbyterian Church in 1976. At that time his findings were surprising and his predictions optimistic. His statistics confirmed our contention about the middle-class status of most African American Presbyterians. He discovered that in terms of per capita giving, years of schooling, membership growth by congregations, and the relative number of professional and support staff positions at local, regional, and national levels of the denomination, African Americans were out in front, proportionately, of most other groups.

Costen wrote: "Perhaps chauvinistically, I am ready to say with great passion that Black Presbyterians are giving to the United Presbyterian Church its finest hour in almost one hundred years. The church needs to know this."

But that was the situation twenty years ago. Since those days the UPCUSA and the Presbyterian Church in the U.S. reunited to form the Presbyterian Church (U.S.A.) of more than three million members. The glowing picture Dr. Costen painted in 1976 has changed considerably since he and his counterpart, Rev. John F. Anderson, Moderator of the 123rd General Assembly of the PCUS, jointly declared that the two divided churches, meeting together for the first time since the Civil War on June 10, 1983, in Atlanta, had ceased to exist separately and a reunited church was aborning. But today the future for African Americans in the new Presbyterian Church (U.S.A.) is doubtful.

Although we have no reliable study of the African American members of the church today, it is very likely, according to our estimate, that we are fewer than the 72,698 Costen reported in 1976. There are also fewer African American staff persons at all levels of the denomination; fewer commissioners at meetings of the General Assembly and the middle judicatories; and a lower morale among us, particularly in the new "integrated presbyteries" of the South where, prior to the 1980s, African American Presbyterians were in control of their own governing bodies. In many respects the situation has changed vastly since the 1980s and, unfortunately, not much of it for the good of the Black constituency.

The lessening of African American participation at the regional and national levels of the church suggests that some of the decline may be due to a cooling off of enthusiasm among both Whites and Blacks for unqualified, one-way racial integration. Matching that decline has been an increased demand from other ethnic minorities and women for equal attention from the church. Add to that other factors that have affected most mainstream denominations in the United States: (1) the widespread attraction of media-driven, charismatic New Age movements and Pentecostalism, which have had a great impact on mainstream church attendance and growth in the African American, Hispanic, and Asian American communities; (2) the acceleration of upward socioeconomic mobility among many African Americans, with its concomitant syndrome of creeping secularization even in the midst of forces pushing in the other direction; (3) ideological and theological ambivalence and confusion, doubt, and a general disinterest in "establishment" religion among all segments of the population.

Can Any Good Thing Come Out of Black Presbyterianism?

It is not yet clear how all of the aforementioned factors have affected African American Presbyterians, but that there has been a decline in both our numbers and participation in the church at all levels few would dispute. Costen's earlier enthusiasm about our contribution to the denomination's health seems out of sync with reality today. Of course, there are still some African American Presbyterian congregations that compare favorably with White sister congregations in terms of the indexes of middle classism—college degrees, good jobs, home ownership, annual income, and money in the bank. Some of us respond to this comparison with pride; others are dismayed. The latter say, because we are no longer in the ranks of the poor and unemployed, how can we be expected to participate in the struggle of most Black people to achieve the American dream? Do we have anything distinctive to offer other than the same indifference toward the poor, the same benign materialism, the same reactionary domestic and foreign policies and general political conservatism that is found among the majority of White Presbyterians?

The question deserves serious consideration. If good jobs, retirement security, homes that are paid for, children in the best colleges, and summer vacations in Europe or cruising the Caribbean disqualify African American Christians for the kind of discipleship we have been discussing in this book, we have been wasting our time reading it. Much of what has been said here about the resources of the tradition will have to be judged anachronistic and irrelevant for Presbyterians.

Critics of bourgeois Christianity would say that we have already accommodated so much to the seduction of corporate America, picking up the profits that fall like savory crumbs from the master's table, that there is no way back. They would contend that liberators of the wretched of the earth must be made of sterner stuff. Not the elite and affluent, but those who are hurting the most—the urban proletariat and the landless farm workers—will lead the fight for social justice.

Because African American Presbyterians are rarely found in the ranks of the truly needy—the welfare mothers, agricultural migrants, petty criminals, the addicted, and the thousands of young Black men now languishing in prisons—we must be considered a part of the problem rather than the solution, part of the system of apathy, greed, and exploitation that grinds the faces of the poor at home and in Africa, Latin America, and Asia.

Whatever one may think of the cogency of this argument, only two clear alternatives seem available to us: (1) either give up the idea of African American Presbyterians' being at the forefront of a revitalization of religion that radically challenges the status quo; (2) or (and this seems equally unlikely) give up the accoutrements of our middle-class status and return to the ghetto to make common cause with the brothers and sisters left behind. There must be other options, but these two are the most often talked about. The first is crushingly pessimistic; the second is fatuously optimistic.

The questions we need to address, and perhaps the most important questions in this book, are the following: Does our faith as African American Presbyterians provide us with anything between these two alternatives? Is it possible that those of us who are no longer at the bottom of the ladder can mount an effective ministry to those who are, and do so without condescension or paternalism and without giving up some of that good life for which we and our parents labored long and hard in the midnight hour?

The Witness of the New Testament

There are no easy answers to these questions. The New Testament teaches that wealth is a snare to the pilgrim who walks among those who have no place to lay their heads. Nothing is harder than for the rich to enter the kingdom of God, yet no one is rejected solely on that account. Evidently there were people of property and wealth among the followers of Jesus. Not many perhaps, but enough to assure us that they were not categorically excluded from the early church. Paul hints at several places that he and his poorest churches depended on the generosity of affluent Christians. There must have been a way to own wealth and property after Pentecost and still be considered a serious and obedient witness to the gospel.

Of course, while we pursue this line of thinking we must be careful not to exaggerate the position of many African American Presbyterians today. There is a big difference between being comfortable and being wealthy by Fortune 500 standards. Like many Americans, we exist on the brink of financial disaster most of our lives and have a vivid memory of what it is like to be really poor. But the fact remains that the gap between our disposable income and that of most people of the world is enormous and getting wider year by year. We are still a highly privileged group, despite the well-known statistical disparity between White and Black.

In the church of Jesus Christ, where "not many were powerful, not many were of noble birth" (1 Cor. 1:26), in a church where the poor heard Jesus gladly because he not only healed their diseases but also reminded them that "yours is the kingdom of God" (Luke 6:20), we who live well will have much to account for when we appear before the judgment seat (Matt. 25:31–46).

Many of our urban churches are located in neighborhoods where people are ill-fed, ill-clothed, and ill-housed, but it is rare when we are involved in ministry to such people on a basis that goes beyond soup kitchens and clothes closets. We need to worry more about how it is possible to please God if we continue to indulge ourselves in the same unconcern and indifference that we have accused White Presbyterians of having toward those who suffer daily privation.

To say that there is no easy way out of this dilemma is not to say that there is nothing that can be done. Jesus called upon the young man to "go, sell your possessions, and give the money to the poor . . . then come, follow me" (Matt. 19:21). However, there is no indication that Jesus made that a general rule for everyone. He did not press the same requirement upon Levi (Luke 5:27–32) or Zacchaeus (Luke 19:1–10), yet both were obviously well off. The same must be said of "the other Mary," the mother of John Mark, whose spacious house in Jerusalem was at the disposal of the disciples (Acts 12:12).

One possibility is John Wesley's advice in his sermon on the use of money, where he says, "Gain all you can, save all you can, give all you can." Another is to live as if having or not having the goods of this world is no issue because we know with the apostle Paul "what it is to have little, and I know what it is to have plenty" (Phil. 4:11–13). That is to say, we know how to use all things and conditions for the glory of God. A contemporary strategy of Christian liberals is to empower the dispossessed so they will be able to throw off their bonds and take responsibility for their own lives. On the other hand, few charitable acts are more risky than to encourage starving people to break the lock on the door of the bread factory—even in the name of the One who said, "I am the bread of life."

In Search of a New Style of Life

If we are serious about what it means to be African American and Presbyterian, we must constantly search for a new style of life that does not ignore the fact that most of us are on the side of the haves rather than the have-nots. We need a new style of being adequately fed and adequately housed in the midst of an ocean of poverty and misery all around us—a new model of service to the world for which Christ died.

By "style" we refer to that distinctive mode of living, of personal conduct and collective action, of characteristic form and function whereby a people demonstrate who they are, what they think of themselves, and what they value in this world.

Artistic and professional people have a style about themselves. For example, a five-star general, a cop directing traffic, a jazz musician, or a Metropolitan Opera diva "walks, talks, and dresses the part" in public. A popular candidate for political office is said to have a "charismatic personality"; a physician is said to have a good "bedside manner." Marcus Garvey, Malcolm X, and Martin Luther King Jr. had distinctive but different lifestyles. Adherents of orthodox Judaism, Hare Krishnas, members of the Society of Friends, the Mennonites, and members of the Church of the Latter-day Saints have different and distinctive styles of life.

Style has to do with communication. People who have a distinctive lifestyle are usually getting across a communiqué, a message of some sort to themselves, to others in their group, and to outsiders. If it is done only in public, it is morally nil. If it is done too self-consciously, it can be a mild irritant to many people. If it is done too naturally, too unself-consciously, it may be received as ambiguity, too enigmatic as to intention as if someone were "taking us for a ride" or "putting us on." Good style has to be skillfully executed, deliberately projected on the screen of the external world, but not disrespectfully. That's why we appreciate what we call good style. But to be "good" it must somehow strike a balance between being morally strict and goody-goody, too flashy and practically invisible, overly studied and "letting it all hang out," as if one couldn't care less about what other people think.

What can be said about the current style of most Presbyterians? Some would say that our style is to have no style. Many of us pride ourselves on being as inconspicuous as possible about our religious commitments. Lest we give the impression that we are fanatical about our faith, we prefer to melt quietly into the great flock of middle-class, decent, law-abiding Americans who are never ostentatious or raise their voices in public, except at a football game. There is nothing wrong with such a lifestyle, except that it's boring. Its communication potential is near zero.

Christians should have more of a lifestyle than this. African American Presbyterians need something different and impressive about the "way we walk," to use that good biblical phrase. We need something to make us stand out from the run-of-the-mill, middle-class American. We need something that communicates what we value and disvalue in life; what we think about ourselves; how we view the world in the light of the gospel filtered through African American Christian sensibilities.

This may sound too crafty and artificial, the substitution of one phoniness for another. But the fact is that today nothing less than an exhibition of difference as opposed to sameness will grasp attention and cause outsiders to ask, "What makes these people tick? What do they know that I don't know, and how can I get my hands on it?" The world will no longer pay much attention to what we *say*. It is looking for a demonstration of the gospel's ability to help people "get a life." People want a pantomime of salvation, not a prime-time commercial.

If African American Presbyterians have anything worth showing each other and the world that is efficacious, in spite of the electronic Babel that assails our eyes and ears, we will have to *live* it out. We will have to live it out with a style and flair that is not affectation but an honest and joyous attitude of mind and spirit that communicates who we are individually and collectively, and why we think our way of life is worth recommending to others.

Does this sound too self-aggrandizing? too given to "denominationalism"? Well, what's wrong with hearing people say, "From the way they live I would guess that they're Presbyterians," or "Only a Presbyterian would take the position she took at that school board meeting," or "If there were more Presbyterians in this neighborhood we could get some things done around here"?

People should notice a difference, and that difference should reflect ethos, the moral and aesthetic evaluation of a group that has a consensus about certain understandings and disciplines of life. We commend our beliefs to others by how we carry ourselves, by the way we worship, study, and act, and especially by the kind of hospitality with which we receive each other and strangers. The world will know us by the things that involve us and the things we refuse to be involved in; by the causes we support and those we refuse to support; by the sacrifices we are willing to make and the spirit with which we make them. All of us have our secrets and little hypocrisies, but petty exceptions do not disprove the rule.

In the past, the manner in which African American Presbyterian churches have been different from the majority of traditional Black churches affected us negatively as far as attractiveness and growth were concerned. In the future, it will be how we are changing and the positive character of that change with respect to image and substance that will draw to our churches those brothers and sisters who themselves are unchurched and looking for a way of being African American and Christian that makes a difference in their personal lives and the world around them.

In chapter 9 we will examine a style of life that can make that difference. We will consider a way of walking through the bewilderment and confusion of the contemporary world that reflects the Black religious tradition we have been exploring and at the same time is open to the best that we have received from our long involvement with the Presbyterian Church.

Of course, there is no prescription written in stone for guaranteeing the kind of discipleship we seek and that the world needs, but let us try to open our minds and hearts and, at least, take a look at one possible mode, one style of being Black and Presbyterian. The way that mode or style gets adopted and implemented is in the company of brothers and sisters who have covenanted to travel in the same direction—that is to say, not in our solitary individuality, but in our religious communities, in our local congregations.

Questions for Discussion

Scripture for Reflection: James 5:1–6

1. Do you agree that bourgeois Christians have accommodated so much to the seduction of corporate America that there is no way back to a unified sense of community?

2. Is it possible for Christians to have both financial wealth and pure religion?

3. Would you consider yourself to be a person who openly shares your faith with others or one who lives a boring faith-sharing life?

4. Do you refer to yourself as *saved?* What images come to your mind as you respond to that question?

5. List three ways that African American Presbyterian churches can improve on our style in order to become inviting to persons who live in our parish communities?

6. What do you think contributed to the decline of African Americans in the Presbyterian Church as members, staff persons, and commissioners after 1976?

W e must discover a way of
living that is different from the

way we live now, and we must discover

it together, in our congregations.

9 Five Areas of Lifestyle Change for Congregations

I s it possible that African American Presbyterians can be known by how we raise our children, use our leisure time, discharge our civic responsibilities, and subordinate our individualism in behalf of group ideals and goals? The world cannot help noticing what kind of employers and employees we make, our different patterns of consumption, our economic ethics, our political participation, our use of power. In short, we have to become a different brand of humanity. We must discover a way of living that is different from the way we live now, and we must discover it together, in our congregations.

These indexes are conditioned by the principles we live by, the guidelines that govern our lives individually and as members of a worshiping community. Some of them I have attempted to spell out here; others I have admittedly been vague about or have left out of the discussion altogether. This book does not pretend to be a catalogue of do's and don'ts, a code of behavior. It is necessary for us to talk about such things against the background of what we have inherited from the past and what we hope for the future. Only when we have developed some consensus about them will a voluntary, internalized style of life begin to emerge that will be truly African American and Presbyterian. In the interest of that discussion, we have some specific suggestions to make in five areas: worship, Christian education, evangelism, outreach into the wider community, and ecumenism.

Worship

Many Presbyterian congregations have already examined their worship services and found them lacking the vitality and excitement of the older tradition. Consequently, it is no longer unusual to find a mixed style of worship in African American Presbyterian churches. Those that are growing and holding on to their young people have a greater emphasis on bodily movement, verve, spontaneous "amens," hand clapping, and other kinds of congregational response. Unlike most of our White churches, for many years Black Presbyterians have included an altar call and, following the sermon, an open invitation for visitors to come forward and join the church. But something new has been added. What we are now calling Afrocentric[1] worship boldly employs percussion instruments, gospel music, spirited preaching, and the enthusiasm seldom found in the worship services of the White Presbyterian congregations that we once regarded as models for what ought to happen at our Sunday morning worship services.

It is not enough, however, to make Afrocentric worship nothing more than a carbon copy of traditional forms in the same way we once copied White Presbyterian worship. The pastor and session should help the congregation become selective about drawing on the past. If we want to be truly Afrocentric, what about elements from the Coptic or Ethiopian Orthodox churches, or hymns and rituals adapted from our many sister Presbyterian churches in the motherland? We should be interested in broadening our worship experience so that it includes meaningful and creative forms from African Christianity and other churches of the two-thirds world. If the World Student Christian Federation and the World Council of Churches can happily introduce these elements into their worship, what hinders the National Black Presbyterian Caucus?

Innovations such as a painting of a Black Christ or images of the Black Madonna and Child on the wall of the chancel will, with careful interpretation, remind the congregation of the universal applicability of Christian symbols particularized in their own cultural context. New-style Black worship should mean a joyous return to the African American spiritual and the best gospel songs and choruses that have become internationally respected art forms. Unfortunately, they have been neglected by many mainstream American congregations that hear only the great classical anthems and organ music.

Some of our clergy have discovered that there is a body of "Black sacred writings": certain memorable passages from David Walker, Martin Delany, Maria Stewart, Frederick Douglass, and others of the antebellum period; the poetry of Countee Cullen, Langston Hughes, and Alice Walker; the words of "Lift Every Voice and Sing"; famous excerpts from the speeches and sermons of Howard Thurman, Mordecai W. Johnson, Malcolm X, and Martin Luther King Jr. Of course, this literature is no substitute for the Bible, but it is the rich deposit of almost four hundred years of African American religion and culture. Our Black sacred writings, which are much more meaningful than some of the commercialized gospel songs young people get ecstatic about these days, ought to have a place in the liturgy of the African American Presbyterian Church.

Imagination and creativity can use Black music, the dance, banners, outdoor processionals, dramatic skits, and poetic recitations in the sanctuary to enrich our worship services. Here we have one of the best opportunities to excite the interest of and educate younger members. Explaining the meaning and purpose of these new liturgical elements will help all of us to think through what we are doing when we worship God and also to discover what possibilities are available to us for celebrating the greatness of Christ. Moreover, there is no better way to enlist and instruct young people than to encourage them to help plan and lead congregational worship.

All this is not to say that there is no longer a place for the quiet, meditative worship style with which many older members of the congregation were brought up. By using variety and experimentation, a skillful worship leader will make sure that the preferences of the elderly saints are not neglected. He or she will not forget that being Afrocentric does not mean that we no longer respect diversity. Precisely the contrary! The Constitution of the church makes it clear that there is no one way that Presbyterians must worship.

Christian Education

An entire book could be written on the educational implications of the new lifestyle of African American Presbyterians. The National Black Presbyterian Caucus (NBPC) has sponsored numerous workshops on the subject, and those reports are available to anyone interested. We cannot explore all those recommendations here. Of course, our primary targets are the children and youth. Over the years the Presbyterian Church has offered church school materials that make glancing references to ethnic minorities, and in 1977 four racial/ethnic minority development offices were established in the Program Agency of the UPCUSA to meet the educational and other needs of minorities. But something more is obviously required. We need a comprehensive curriculum that integrates the church school, youth groups, adult classes, camps and conference programs, and church-sponsored supplements to public education around the central themes of what we have called the African American Christian tradition. The denomination must also stop politely tolerating such materials if we want to pick up the check for their publication. It must authorize, publish, and aggressively promote them in collaboration with NBPC.

What does it mean to identify oneself as both an African American and a Christian? What is meant by a new lifestyle for men, women, and children who are discovering their ancestors and themselves in African and African

American history and want to use what they have learned in Christian worship and action? Several denominations have produced educational resources that attempt to answer these questions, but none has been notably successful in getting them used by local congregations.

Some years ago the United Presbyterian Church introduced the Faith Journey series to its African American congregations, but it was poorly prepared for and lacked the promotional pressure with which the denomination marketed its standard Christian Faith and Life curriculum. It deserved equal treatment, but did not get it.

Many congregations have introduced Afrocentric material by having lectures on history and theology coincide with their annual revivals, weekend family camps, or all-day Saturday church conferences. Brief, interesting talks, films, or skits followed by small-group discussions for feedback and interspersed with spirited singing can accomplish more over a six- or eight-hour period or at an overnight retreat than a month of hurried church school lessons about African American biblical studies or the history of Christianity in Africa and the Caribbean.

Although the emphasis should be on children and young people, adult education must not be neglected, and in many cases it will be necessary to educate the parents before many of them will permit access to their children. Ideally, all grades, using the same core curriculum, should proceed simultaneously. All material used should interface and reinforce each graded part and any other material that the denomination produces in a congregationwide program of Christian education. Indeed, a basic attribute of new-style African American Presbyterianism will be the attention it gives to continuous, creative educational experiences for the entire congregation. We have to become again a reading, writing, and dialogic church—from the primary grades to the adult Bible class. That, after all, is a part of the African American Presbyterian tradition that has come down to us from our forebears.

There is too much ignorance of the classics of African American religion and culture—Du Bois's *The Souls of Black Folk*, St. Clair Drake's *The Redemption of Africa and Black Religion*, Carter G. Woodson's *The Mis-Education of the Negro*, Howard Thurman's *Jesus and the Disinherited*, Benjamin Mays's *With Heart and Head*, and James H. Cone's *A Black Theology of Liberation*—to mention only a few. African American Christians who do not read do not know this literature and, therefore, are woefully uninformed about the rock from which they were hewn. One could safely wager that they get their cues about lifestyle from the prime-time television sitcoms and *Jet* magazine. Both may be useful for taking the pulse of the times, but they are no substitute for a systematic program of Christian education that focuses on the reading of the classic texts of the Black world.

By a "reading, writing, and dialogic church" we mean one consisting of families and individuals who set great store in preserving and passing on African American history, theology, and literature, as well as the Bible. A church that has an active lending library, a book-review club, a committee researching local church history, and dialogue groups that discuss topics that run the gamut from the current trends in womanist theology to the latest novel by John Edgar Wideman. A reading, writing, and dialogic congregation is already on the way to a new Afrocentric lifestyle through Christian education.

Evangelism

African American churches have traditionally emphasized evangelism. The sawdust trail is all too familiar to us. The mourner's bench, the annual week of revival (now often reduced to three days), and the pastor's call for a decision, followed by "opening the doors of the church" for repentant sinners are standard fare for traditional Black congregations. But evangelism in new-style congregations has a broader and deeper meaning. It should have to do not only with introducing men, women, and children to Jesus Christ by convicting them of their sin and unworthiness before God, but also by showing those who ask the jailer's question to Paul and Silas, "Sirs, what must I do to be saved?" (Acts 16:30) the revelatory meaning of the African American religious experience that comes from the depths and breaks the surface of our literature, art, music, and folklore.

That experience of peoplehood, of solidarity in suffering and struggle, becomes the context for evangelism insofar as the inquirer is able to identify with those who have gone before and, on the strength of their testimony, is constrained to begin his or her own journey toward liberation and reconciliation.

God is always seeking us as individuals who need to be "saved," but the African American experience is that we are found, not in our solitariness, but in our solidarity with those with whom we share the stony road and the chastening rod. Those who have traveled that road together and felt that rod on their backs find in the Bible sufficient evidence that God elects and commissions some people to a mission only they can perform, and entrusts them with his purposes for others. Everyone who is led to the belief that he or she is called to that mission is summoned not ultimately as an individual but as a team member, a pilgrim in a company of pilgrims, a soldier in the army.

What that calling is all about in detail, what its special claims are and how we should respond today to them, is what we mean by a new-style evangelism. It may begin with John 3:16 and "Just As I Am," but it goes far beyond those customary power tools of old-style evangelism. It has to do with the Christian life as a whole conformed to the mission of the African American church in its peculiar situation. If we are too ignorant, indifferent, or lazy to pursue that kind of evangelism, we belong to a congregation that may be packed to the rafters with people but is useless as far as the kingdom is concerned.

Despite how negative it may sound, this is not to deprecate traditional ways of pleading, admonishing, challenging, and beguiling people to "accept Jesus as their personal Savior." The invitation in the traditional Black liturgy, with its overpowering sense of urgency, its unabashed emotionalism, and its skillful use of music and bodily movement is truly a "moving experience" and needed in many staid African American Presbyterian churches. But there is more to the tradition, much more. There is no reason why other methods of bringing people to Christ cannot be used as well—from the open-air street meetings that African American Presbyterians in Philadelphia sponsored during the days of Rev. John Gloucester and his sons, to the cultivation of prospective converts through "proselytes of the gate" groups, where people participate, without specific commitment, in a "soft periphery" that focuses primarily on something other than hard-core organized religion—for example, on Black history and culture.

Today, African American Presbyterian churches are not growing at a rate that even begins to keep pace with the African American population. Some observers predict that, given the closing of our churches and the dearth of new church developments, at some point in the twenty-first century there will be virtually no African American Presbyterians left in the United States. If this is a probability, we are challenged to disprove the prediction by concentrating on the right kind of evangelism and church-growth strategies.

The desperate search for live bodies to fill the pews and swell the offering plates can vulgarize the most enthusiastic evangelism program and must be avoided. Nor should numbers alone make us think that our churches will continue into the remote future. It is possible for African American Presbyterianism to be snuffed out without any evidence of having ever existed if we insist on being nothing more than religious theaters for people who want to see a good show and have a high old time. We need to be evangelists who help people catch a vision of what it means to be a follower of Christ as a new-style African American Presbyterian.

This suggests the other equally important aspect of evangelism—the nurture of new converts. It is a common experience to sign persons up only to see them fall away during the succeeding months. New-style evangelism will require that old members agree to sponsor and follow up new members. When they are drawn into families and intimate face-to-face groups, when we stop by to pick them up for church or pray with them as they face the lonely task of taking up the yoke of Christ, we will find fewer new members straying to other churches. There is nothing novel about this kind of care and feeding of converts, but many fashionable churches have not been able to lay this burden for souls on their members. It will take a commitment to a new style of "growing churches" to make our congregations evangelistic in the best sense of that term.

The issue of class discrimination cannot be evaded here. It is a problem in many mainstream Black churches. As the lady in Hattiesburg said, "Pedestrians be too high class" for many poor folks who live in the shadow of our churches. Whether justified or not, a poor reputation precedes us in the streets. Because of the general rise of African Americans into a lower middle-class status, the situation is not as deplorable as it was thirty years ago. However, it is still true that we are considered exclusive. Many of our congregations seldom present themselves in a favorable light to the community, and as a result large segments of the community never think about visiting a Presbyterian church. The word is out that "those classy folks just think they're better than anybody else."

The impression may be sadly mistaken, but it persists nevertheless. One of the reasons for adopting a new style is to break through this reputation and demonstrate that we are people who not only practice hospitality but also welcome all our neighbors to explore with us an exciting new form of African American Christianity.

Evangelism has to do with the totality of the Christian commitment—the proclamation and demonstration of the power of God to redeem persons, groups, and institutions. The new-member class is a critical place for evangelism. We commend a new-style discipleship to people whenever we help them to see that joining our church means many things—from learning how to pray, to reading the Bible with the spectacles of African American biblical scholars, to working in a study group that investigates drug addiction or Black-on-Black crime. When a new member presents herself or himself to answer the constitutional questions, she or he should receive a voter's registration card, a map showing the socioeconomic characteristics of the neighborhood, a book on African American history and culture, as well as an inclusive-language Bible, and an assigned place in a dialogue group, as well as a packet of Sunday offering envelopes. There is no discipleship without discipline.

The time is past when we can give people the idea that all it takes to be a member of one of our congregations is to believe in Christ and pay their pledge. We are a people on the move to the kingdom of God. Those who join us on this journey come without racial, class, gender, or any other qualification. They must be prepared to have Christ change their lives! Because they are becoming new Presbyterians, they must also be willing to consider what that change will look like not only in interracial settings but also in the context of a poor, needful, and often isolated African American community.

Outreach into the Wider Community

Throughout this discussion we have been concerned with the middle-class bias of the African American constituency of the Presbyterian Church and whether it is reasonable to expect people like us ever to play a significant role in the empowerment of poor people. Have we so shielded ourselves from the African American Christian tradition of redemptive suffering through the struggle that it is too late to change? Or can we begin now to forge a new style of life that will reach out to the world around us? One thing seems certain, and we ought not deceive ourselves about it. African American Presbyterians who have worked hard and honestly all their lives to provide themselves and their children with a modicum of what it takes to live in this world (with a hedge against the worst ravages of racism and poverty) are not likely to give up everything in the interest of some visionary proposal for social improvement by means of personal divestment. We are no different from anybody else when it comes to rationalizing our advantages and finding reasons for substituting a cup of cold water for transformations that require redistributing wealth and power. But this does not mean folding our arms around us in our stained-glass foxholes and watching the weary world go by.

Christians must always challenge themselves and others to transcend the selfishness of the unredeemed world—even when the prospects for 100 percent success are meager. God continually surprises us by grace. On the other hand, the serpentine wisdom of Christ's followers (Matt. 10:16), ought to make secular men and women who believe the gospel find ways of transforming the environment in order to transform behavior, as well as the other way around.

We are not certain of all that was in our Lord's mind when he bade his followers to "make friends for yourselves by means of dishonest wealth" (Luke 16:9). However, he seems to have been giving practical counsel in the interest of a kingdom that was as earthly conditioned as it was heaven-bound. We have already noted that people immersed in the cultures of Africa and of Africa-in-America are not surprised or shocked by such revelations of Christian shrewdness. We are no strangers to this kind of holy worldliness.

For the most part, our churches are in the African American community. We are part and parcel of that scene, whether we like it or not. We stand or fall with others in that community. Even after we relocate to a more affluent, residential ring or to the suburbs, it would behoove us to keep our connection with those persons and institutions that remain in the old neighborhood. We need to reach out to brothers and sisters left behind, to take leadership in community organizations and agencies that are in search of a better life for everyone in the city. It is understandable why nobody would want to return to an impoverished ghetto, but it is neither Christian nor prudent to try to exist indefinitely on an island surrounded by poisoned waters when something can be done about the pollution.

Aside from their expected compassion and sense of moral purpose, the self-interest of our congregations should make them move out into the community, not just to operate a clothes closet for the naked or a hot-lunch program for the hungry, but to help both groups register and vote, find work and housing, present themselves regularly at City Hall to link up with other forces working to raise the level of expectation, aspiration, and effectiveness of poor people in bringing about social, economic, and political change. If we do find ourselves living on an island of prosperity surrounded by a sea of misery, it is our duty not only to widen that island but also to purify those waters so that life can blossom and flourish everywhere.

The real key to a missional style of life is not the old-fashioned social action committee of a local congregation but the broad involvement of the whole people with secular organizations, community institutions, and governmental agencies. There is no point in reinventing the wheel. In most communities it is not a question of starting something new but of getting seriously engaged in what is already going on to raise the quality of life and change whatever needs changing. Some congregations have built family life or neighborhood centers in which counseling services, day care, senior citizen programs, and many other secular services can be housed in close contact with the resources of the congregation. Thus outreach to the wider community is reinforced by inreach to the members, enlisting them in voluntary services with agencies that sorely need citizen participation to keep them honest and responsible to the people, rather than to some fossilized bureaucracy downtown.

Ecumenism

Ecumenism is an area that is usually given superficial attention on the national and international level but is neglected altogether by many congregations on the local level. It is closely related to outreach in cooperation with secular community organizations. The problem in the African American community is not that Black Christians are uninvolved in the good things that are going on. We are probably more involved than any other group of laypersons in the community. The problem is that we are often out there as discrete and theologically disoriented individuals. When it comes to a corporate, ecumenical witness, informed by the insights and discernments of Black theology, we are immature and dissociated from one another. The mark of a new style of life on the part of our congregations will be a more aggressive effort to call on and establish strong ties with traditional Black churches in our areas to work out ways of sharing material and human resources for outreach.

It is true that African American Baptists and Pentecostals can be clannish; African Methodists are constantly caught up in a whirlwind of denominational activities; and African American churches of other predominantly White denominations are as class conscious and recessive as Presbyterians. But someone needs to take the initiative and encourage churches in urban neighborhoods to pool what they have for the good of all. The Congress of National Black Churches, headquartered in Washington, D.C., has been emphasizing this, but the message has not seeped down to the grass roots.

African American churches are woefully nonecumenical. We visit each other, exchange pulpits and choirs, meet irregularly at ministerial associations and during crises in the community. But we show little interest in sharing on a day-to-day basis what the apostle Paul, in 1 Corinthians 12, calls our varieties of spiritual gifts. What he has to say about individual brothers and sisters applies equally to churches: "For just as the body is one and has many members, and all the members of the body, though many, are one body, so it is with Christ. For in the one Spirit we were all baptized into one body—Jews or Greeks, slaves or free—and we were all made to drink of one Spirit" (1 Cor. 12:12–13).

Ecumenism challenges us to something more than interchurch fellowship. Sharing the varieties of spiritual gifts that have been cultivated in the histories of each denomination requires that we get to know one another at a much deeper level than visits by neighboring choirs and annual union services on Good Friday. Ecumenism requires that we dialogue about our gifts, our theologies, our testimonies; that we describe to each other our pilgrim journey and the vision of the kingdom toward which we move separately and together; that we go out hand in hand to meet the One who goes before us into "haunts of wretchedness and need"; and that we regularly share the one loaf of bread that is Christ's body, the one cup of salvation, and the one continual quest for the "unity of the Spirit in the bond of peace" (Eph. 4:3).

Black ecumenism is not a luxury we can afford only after the Baptists have had their several anniversaries, the Methodists have exhausted their quota of district conferences and all the other meetings in between, the Pentecostals have had enough of the Holy Spirit that they can pay attention to something else for a change, and the Presbyterians have done all things "decently and in order" that the presbytery and the Louisville offices have mandated. Black ecumenism is the *sine qua non* of everything we needed in the 1960s and need today—no less urgently. Everything that cannot be most effectively implemented by churches working alone must be done together: Black economic development, communitywide campaigns against the drug trade and other vices, pressure on law enforcement and judicial process agencies, ministry to prisoners and parolees, a quasi-independent African American political base, alternative schools, family counseling centers, consumer cooperatives and credit unions, and regular financial assistance for the local, national, and international causes we all profess to believe in.

The issues are too large and complex and the problems too demanding for each of us to waste time and energy trying to dredge a river with a plastic dipper. We need each other's labor and encouragement. We need the spiritual gifts and the presence and power of brothers and sisters from different traditions to minister in these times. This new-style ecumenism will have one Presbyterian congregation regularly worshiping, studying, planning, and acting with at least two or three congregations of other denominations in the neighborhood. One pastor must have enough vision, theological perspective, and discipline to take the initiative—spurning rebuff, indifference, and criticism—to open up a discussion, first in his or her own congregation and then with others, about the visible unity in faith and mission of the whole church of Christ.

Moreover, we cannot escape the question about an ecumenism that includes our White brothers and sisters and those from other ethnic groups. The emphasis we have just made about bonding with African American churches does not, by any means, relieve us from ecumenical relations with White and interracial congregations, in addition to congregations of other ethnic minorities.

Although White congregations of the Presbyterian Church and of other denominations will continue to decline numerically in the inner city, we can anticipate an increasing number of predominantly White churches that will seek more than a token integration of African American individuals and families. Many will be found in changing inner-city neighborhoods, but many will be in fairly stable suburban areas.

There is no reason for us to fear this development. Every community should have at least one model of authentic racial integration in the Christian church for those who feel called to such a fellowship and witness. Indeed, the long-range future of the church and the world is obviously not separatism but increasing unity and integration. Presbyterians who exhibit the new lifestyle we have been exploring will have no difficulty attending a monoracial congregation on one day and a biracial or multiracial congregation on another—and expecting all three pastors to understand what we are doing and why.

Interracial ecumenism is not a routine affair that requires merely good intentions on all sides. It requires dialogue, that is, speaking the truth in love. White Christians, after all these years, need to understand why we can accept them as brothers and sisters and still fight them whenever they need to be opposed. They cannot understand this without knowing something about the history and ethos of the African American church and community. How that learning takes place, and what Whites should do with it once it is acquired, is a complicated question that deserves more discussion than we can have here. It must be said, however, that Whites need to expose themselves to "Blackenization" no less than they have always expected us to "act White" in order to be accepted into the mainstream.

We are not talking about hand-clapping, body-swaying, speech-slurring, foot-stomping, and eyeball-rolling behavior—the Sambo-like imitation that some Whites call "really gettin' down with Black folks." They must have a keen sensitivity and willingness to be immersed in the values of African American religion and culture without the necessity of making it their own. It involves directed observation, reading, listening, entering into worship and discussion with African Americans more than once or twice a year. Covenanting ecumenical arrangements with African American congregations will sooner or later suggest issues that crisscross the two communities and call for joint strategy and action.

Perhaps it is to be expected that we could not have been isolated from one another for centuries and expect ecumenism across race and class lines to develop quickly and easily. We have to proceed with deliberate speed with a few people on both sides who are mature enough, sincere enough, and prepared enough to take risks; people who are willing to trust the Holy Spirit to bring operational unity out of years of de facto and de jure disunity, and mutual forgiveness out of mutual guilt and incrimination; people who believe that Christian love can cover a multitude of mistakes and sins on both sides.

All this is to say that new-style African American Presbyterianism involves a new posture toward the Blacks in the ghetto and the Whites in suburbia. It will be neither paternalistic, nor standoffish, nor slavishly accommodating to either group. Eyeball to eyeball, it will discuss and negotiate reciprocal relations in behalf of liberation and reconciliation understood as two sides of a single coin. The new style involves working in partnership with those from whom we have been estranged, for the hard truth is that we sometimes have more in common with White folks than we do with some Black folks. Skin color has never guaranteed anything and, never will.

The partnership we seek is not "for social caucusing," "for fun and fellowship," "to show poor folks what great gals and guys we are," or "for getting White folks straightened out once and for all." Rather, it is to enter into a quest for the unity of the body of Christ across every barrier that separates us today.

That is a formidable challenge indeed! Is it possible that we can go together into the world, fully cognizant of our differences of attitude, background, culture, theological perspective, even mission priorities, and yet work out those differences and others as we go?

For some of us the answer to that question is no, or at least it is clouded in uncertainty. Those who have been attentive to what has been going on in our churches since the reunion are aware that in the last few years a profound question has been raised by some African American Presbyterians. It has to do with whether we can be truly ourselves, truly Afrocentric, and remain in the same denomination with White people. It is to that question we turn in the final chapter of this book.

Questions for Discussion

Scripture for Reflection: James 2:1–10

1. Have you ever considered leaving the Presbyterian Church? If so, list two reasons you have decided to remain.

2. Would your congregation be resistant to incorporating Afrocentric music or study materials into your style of worship and Bible study? What are some ways that this transition could be made easier? Would it be easier to accomplish this by having a second service? Is your congregation willing to absorb the additional cost of a second service?

3. Do you think that the increasing number of African American Presbyterian clergywomen will have a positive or negative effect on the future of this denomination? Why or why not?

4. How would you react if someone who smelled or looked bad sat next to you in church?

5. Can African American Presbyterian churches effectively partner with other denominations, European churches, or churches of other races until we have come to terms with our own identity?

I n any case, we can agree that after 190 years of African American Presbyterian history, square one is no place to be.

10   Is This New Wine?

In December 1992, a group of African American Presbyterian ministers and lay people met with the late Mildred Brown, then the Associate for Racial and Cultural Diversity of the church's national staff, to consider many of the questions we have tried to address in this book. The purpose of the group, called the African American Advisory Committee, was to advise the national staff and our constituency on what the committee perceived to be the extreme crisis in which African American members of the Presbyterian Church (U.S.A.) stand in this final decade of the twentieth century.

According to another national staff person, Dr. Otis Turner, the meeting was a *kairos* moment. The Greek word suggests a time laden with meaning and decisiveness. It was an intensely critical moment when the harsh realities of our past and present experience in the Presbyterian Church collided with unprecedented force with the new Afrocentric consciousness of many of our younger and more active pastors and laypersons to demand a resolution of an extreme dilemma. The dilemma of being, at one and the same time, both conscientious African American Presbyterians, eager to reclaim our past and envision a new future, and loyal members of this overwhelmingly White and sometimes insensitive Presbyterian Church (U.S.A.).

Dr. Turner, describing that kairotic moment, writes: "There was agony; there was pain; there was praying; there was singing; there was reflection; there was celebration; and there was God. And something happened. Is it new wine?"

The allusion to wine recalls a parable of Jesus that is found in all three of the Synoptic Gospels. When our Lord was questioned about the moral inflexibility of the Pharisees compared with the freedom of his own followers, he responded: "Neither is new wine put into old wineskins; otherwise, the skins burst, and the wine is spilled, and the skins are destroyed; but new wine is put into fresh wineskins, and so both are preserved" (Matt. 9:17; cf. Mark 2:22 and Luke 5:37–38).

At its 1992 meeting, the African American Advisory Committee drafted a remarkable document titled "Is This New Wine? A Paper for Discussion Among African American Presbyterians," which concludes with a vision of a new, vibrant church in the United States called the African Presbyterian Church in America (APCA).

Like Dr. Martin Luther King Jr., the committee had a dream. It dreamed that in the year 2052 the APCA would be a full-fledged denomination of some 575 congregations and 1.75 million members; that it would have separated itself from an obsolescent Presbyterian Church (U.S.A.) at the beginning of the twenty-first century; and that it would be bringing together the African diaspora in all parts of the North and South Atlantic and the Caribbean into one international African American communion. The result would be a truly Afrocentric Presbyterian denomination admirably suited for a great heritage and the difficult but exhilarating challenges of the Black world in the western hemisphere.

The document, referred to as "Is This New Wine?" sets forth some of the reasons for this independent church and the process needed to ascertain the readiness of African American members of the Presbyterian Church (U.S.A.) to entertain this brave new vision and bring it into reality. A group calling itself Presbyterians for Prayer, Study, and Action was set up "to present this matter for the prayerful reflection and debate of all sessions of predominantly African American congregations and their congregations."[1] A seven-year period, beginning in August 1993, was recommended for a national study and discussion process. According to Part VI of the paper, titled "Where To from Here? Conclusions and Recommendations for Action," published in April 1993, that process should include the following:

1. Development of appropriate theological reflection regarding concepts raised in this paper.

2. Adoption of a national goal calling for the establishment of at least five new African American Presbyterian congregations annually over the next seven years.

3. Funds set aside ($500 annually) by all existing African American Presbyterian congregations for support of new church development in African American communities, as well as by individuals able to do so.

4. Establishment of New Church Development Leadership Teams (a paradigm for new church development that includes the pastor, secretarial support, and a musician with skills in Afrocentric musicianship).

5. Outlining of regional organizational and administrative structures.[2]

It is concerning this vision of a new Presbyterian church, the rationale behind it, and the implementing proposals, that Presbyterians for Prayer, Study, and Action, which now sponsors the revised 1992 document, asks, "Is This New Wine?" If the answer is yes, the significance of our Lord's parable becomes obvious. New wine requires fresh wineskins so that both the wine and the wineskins may be preserved. If the answer is no, we go back to square one. Feminist theologian Letty Russell, however, suggests another possibility when she asks, "What happens to old wineskins when you try to make them contain new wine?" Her piquant remark deserves consideration. There is a difference between starting something brand new and forcing renewal on something old.

A Time for Decision

In any case, we can agree that after 190 years of African American Presbyterian history, square one is no place to be. The group that entreats us to pray about, study, and take action on their proposal by the year 2000 should be thanked for forcing Black Presbyterians to stop drifting aimlessly through this church and make some careful judgments about who we are and the mission to which we have been called as African American Christians. It is too late in the day for equivocation. Throughout this book we have recommended a serious biblical, historical, and theological audit of where we have come from and where we are today. "Is This New Wine?" intends to encourage precisely that kind of investigation.

We have talked about a viable Christian tradition that is not only worth preserving but, if it can be conveyed in a new style of life that enhances its values, may be the springboard we need to catapult us out of our doldrums. "Is This New Wine?" is one among other documents of Black Presbyterian caucuses that are concerned to promote that tradition and new lifestyle.

There is, therefore, a sense in which the "Is This New Wine?" proposal for deep study and daring action is not altogether unprecedented. Black Presbyterians United (BPU), the national organization that preceded the present National Black Presbyterian Caucus (NBPC), challenged the African American constituency to shake the foundations of conventional Presbyterianism by reforming itself from within and returning to the community with a radical form of discipleship shaped by Black liberation theology and African spirituality. NBPC itself has carried on that tradition.

Nevertheless, the crowning vision of the "Is This New Wine?" document—withdrawal from the Presbyterian Church, as the possible result of seven years of prayer and study, in order to form a new denomination by the year 2000—*is* new and unprecedented. Of course, in years past we heard halfhearted suggestions for forming a Black Presbyterian church or uniting with the Second Cumberland Presbyterian Church, a small all-Black denomination in the mid-South. Yet this is the first time that African American Presbyterian leaders, drawn from both the old southern and northern branches of the denomination, have asked us to decide whether or not we can be Afrocentric Christians and remain in this reunited church—whether it is possible to be Black and Presbyterian at this point in history without having our own African American denomination.

It is a serious and inescapable challenge. We owe sincere thanks to everyone who took part in drafting and publishing a document that raises such a question with a thoughtfulness and passion with which it has never been raised before. The roll call of the drafters and presenters is too long to include here, but a few key people need to be mentioned for the record.

The list includes Mildred Brown; Professor Ronald E. Peters, Pittsburgh Theological Seminary; Rev. Robert Burkins, Elmwood Presbyterian Church in East Orange, New Jersey; Professor Warren Dennis, New Brunswick Theological Seminary in New Jersey; Rev. Amitiyah Elayne Hyman, New York Avenue Presbyterian Church in Washington, D.C.; Professor Marsha Snulligan Haney, Interdenominational Theological Center in Atlanta; and Dr. Lonnie Oliver, New Life Presbyterian Church in Atlanta. These are only a few of the many people across the nation who have devoted prayerful time and effort to bring this important matter before the African American members of this church.

It is indeed time for a decision. Nothing has been laid before us in this century that states the issues more urgently and prepares us more carefully to decide who we are and where we belong. Although some of the people in the pews have not yet read the "Is This New Wine?" paper, it has probably received a wider readership and discussion than any study document ever recommended to African American Presbyterian congregations. If by the year 2000 we are not ready to respond to its challenge, the fault will be that our pastors and sessions have been too lax with their leadership responsibilities or too rigidly disinclined to share "Is This New Wine?" with their congregations; it will not be the fault of the original drafters or Presbyterians for Prayer, Study, and Action.

The Basic Argument of "Is This New Wine?"

The recommendations of Part VI, cited above, make clear that the basic argument of the document is that African American Presbyterianism is in its death throes unless something is done early in the new century that will prevent it from disappearing from the pages of church history. Moreover, it appears to the drafters of "Is This New Wine?" that the Presbyterian Church (U.S.A.) is neither willing nor prepared to do anything decisive about this doleful situation.

Black Presbyterian congregations are experiencing dwindling numbers, decaying physical plants, and vacant pulpits with the result that many presbyteries are closing more and more Black congregations and starting none. It has been noted that an upsurge in the initiation of new churches is reflected nationwide throughout the Presbyterian Church (U.S.A.) in every racial group except among African Americans.

Closely related to this institutional anxiety about the future of our congregations is a deeper concern for the African American community as a whole. This is not an expression of ecclesiastical nervousness about simply preserving and multiplying Black congregations for their own sake. It is about preserving and multiplying Black congregations for the sake of the community. Such a witness will require, according to "Is This New Wine?" a drastic revision of how we think about ourselves and the priority we place on our mission to our own people.

This is not to suggest that merely the initiation of new congregations is needed. Also needed are efforts that will enable existing African American congregations to address more effectively the critical issues of economic blight and educational, social, and political disenfranchisement of their parishioners. Many Black Presbyterian congregations, however, view themselves as being so middle class in their orientations and imitative of what they view as proper "White Presbyterian" liturgy and ethos that they do not relate effectively to other Blacks.

As one reads through "Is This New Wine?" it becomes increasingly evident that the central contention has to do with the value of Afrocentrism and the nagging suspicion that this view, which makes African culture and religion the ground of a Presbyterian theological perspective, can never be successfully inculcated and practiced so long as we remain encapsulated in a predominantly White denomination.

African American Presbyterians need to make up their minds on this question, and the "Is This New Wine?" paper gives us ample opportunity to do just that. In an address to the Midwest Regional of the National Black Presbyterian Caucus in September 1994, Otis Turner made clear what he sees to be at the heart of the proposal to leave the Presbyterian Church (U.S.A.).

We cannot liberate ourselves until we first see ourselves as host to the values that are part of the structures of oppression. Many of the perks and rewards we get from dependency on oppressive structures and for accommodating ourselves to them are things that we ultimately must give up if we are to be free. It is better to walk on our own with a limp than to be carried in style. It is not the limp that is the problem; it is a frame of mind that disposes one to be dependent rather than self-sufficient. The essence of oppression is not physical; it is psychological and spiritual. The essence of liberation is likewise not physical; it is psychological and spiritual. This is why the Afrocentric movement is so critical to our future.

What Is Afrocentrism?

The Afrocentric movement in the United States is too broad and complex to occupy us at sufficient length in these closing pages. However, in brief it is an effort on the part of African Americans to disengage from the worldview and values that place Europe and North America at the center of the universe.

Afrocentrism urges us to find our center of meaning and value in things African. In his influential book *The Afrocentric Idea*, Molefi Kete Asante, regarded by many as the founder of Afrocentrism, writes this:

> My objective has always been a critique that propounds a cultural theory of society by the very act of criticism. In other words, to provide a radical assessment of a given reality is to create, among other things, another reality. . . . I have the insight that comes from being born black in the United States. . . . The crystallization of this critical perspective I have named *Afrocentricity*, which means, literally, placing African ideals at the center of any analysis that involves African culture and behavior.[3]

But the view of Warren Dennis, a Presbyterian minister and professor of urban studies, as well as one of the drafters of "Is This New Wine?" is closer to our interests in this book. Dennis argues that Afrocentrism is a "method of inquiry" into ultimate questions about who we are as Black Presbyterians; this inquiry, therefore, can be a means to reclaiming our cultural, historical, and spiritual heritage by obliging us to relate the gospel more closely to the present situation in our communities.

> As a method of inquiry [Afrocentrism] asks the question, how do we gather meaning out of African or other existence? ... Afrocentrism becomes the source of regeneration for our true values and beliefs grounded in a method of inquiry and discernment. ... By lifting up Afrocentrism as a method of exploration, the centrality of African ideas, beliefs, and values as valid frames of reference for acquiring and examining historical and biblical data for truth and accuracy is established. *Afrocentrism then is a picture of the way things are actually represented in our most comprehensive ideas of nature, self, and society. It is the composite montage of specific ways of thinking, feeling, and acting, which is peculiar to African Americans in general, and African American Presbyterians in particular as distinguished from other groups.*[4]

Warren Dennis and Ronald Peters, another Presbyterian minister and professor at Pittsburgh Theological Seminary, are two of the principal drafters and proponents of the "Is This New Wine?" document. Both are convinced that the only way we can hope to be Afrocentric Christians is to shed the imitative middle-classism of White Presbyterians that has so destroyed our evangelistic capability in the ghetto and to serve the social, political, and economic needs of urban Blacks. That is to say, we need to come out of the Presbyterian Church (U.S.A.) and form a new African Presbyterian Church in America (APCA). Some of our "best and brightest" pastors and lay people across the nation agree, although one suspects that most African American members in the pews have not yet given the matter the serious consideration it deserves.

To the extent that "Is This New Wine?" will force unthinking and indifferent members to ask the questions it raises about Afrocentrism, middle-classism, and social witness in the Black community, it is nothing less than a God-sent blessing, a *kairos* document that is exceptional in the 190-year history of African American Presbyterianism.

Is Total Separation Feasible or Necessary?

Cynicism has no honorable place in this discussion, but it is difficult to imagine how African American Presbyterians, in our present state of theological mis-education, ecclesiastical unconnectedness, and poor stewardship of causes beyond the local congregation, will be able to create and support a national structure that is both strong and recognizably Presbyterian. Of course, it is possible for the congregations of the proposed African Presbyterian Church in America to be so loosely affiliated and unstructured beyond the local congregation that the burden of supporting a national church would be minimal. But in what sense would such a church be Presbyterian, and what happens, under such an arrangement, to the putative emphasis on an international ethnic identity and a transnational unity?

So the question of feasibility is inescapable. It has to do with such practical matters as the cost of putting a denomination in the field that will encompass the North, the South, Central America, and the Caribbean, and of providing the kind of capital investments and other endowments that will be able to maintain a denominational structure over the long haul. Very few of us have any experience operating a national church, so there would have to be an extended period of training. With the dearth of African American men and women seeking ordination or even membership in our churches, it would take many years before a cadre of proficient administrative and program personnel could be formed.

Some will scoff at these rationalizations and say that with faith and determination African Americans are perfectly capable of establishing their own church and the ecclesiastical superstructure that must go with it; that we have among us the talent and financial resources to do almost anything we want to do. Both contentions may be true. There is only one way to find out. What "Is This New Wine?" really wants to determine is how much we are committed to what is being proposed.

Perhaps it is not being too pessimistic to suggest that, given what we know about the consciousness and morale of African American Presbyterians today, there are serious questions about the feasibility of launching a brand-new Presbyterian church made up primarily of the existing Black clergy and lay people. If the situation were otherwise, this book would not have been necessary in the first place.

But the second question is more fundamental: Is it *necessary* for Black Presbyterians to form an autonomous, freestanding, primarily Black denomination in order to be Afrocentric, identified with the poor and oppressed in our communities, and actively engaged in the social, economic, and political action that can contribute to a higher quality of life for our people?

This is what should be at the heart of the debate that we hope will take place in African American congregations during the remaining few years of this century. A reliable answer will require a carefully planned dialogue among us, backed up more by hard facts than rhetorical incrimination and between us and the White majority of the church. We need to be sure what White Presbyterians are prepared to permit (for it is no mystery who will have the votes in General Assembly) and what they refuse to permit us to say and do and still remain in the denomination. In other words, we need to find out what the denomination, from the General Assembly to the local presbyteries, is prepared to commit in terms of polity, program, and financial resources to help us and other ethnic minorities realize our aspirations as Presbyterians who want to preserve and enhance our separate identities *within* a truly interracial and multicultural church. We have no certain idea today what that commitment is or if it even exists in the church to which we now belong.

If after careful and comprehensive negotiations with our White brothers and sisters it becomes evident that being Presbyterian today requires traveling a one-way street toward the kind of racial integration in which theological stance, liturgical practice, ideological orientation, and programmatic involvement must be White, middle class, theologically conservative, and exclusively Eurocentric, then we need not to get out of Presbyterianism—just out of the Presbyterian Church (U.S.A.)! On the other hand, if such discussions prove that our White fellow Presbyterians can tolerate a certain amount of heterodoxy in all things considered nonessential so far as the historic creeds are concerned; if they are willing to accept among us a certain independent, Afrocentric style of faith and order, life and mission; and if they are willing to share the resources of the denomination with us and other ethnic groups that seek a similar centeredness in their own culture, then why should we leave?

All of this depends, in the first place, on how serious we are about engaging in such discussions, saying what we mean and meaning what we say. Such discussions have never been held before now, and none of us knows the answers to these questions. Nor is it likely that we, as African American Presbyterians, are ready to enter into such explorations in our present disorganized state. One might go even further and argue that we must, at the same time, be in dialogue with Presbyterian brothers and sisters on the continent of Africa (after all, we're talking about creating an African church!) and with Native American, Asian American, and Hispanic American Presbyterians. The "Is This New Wine?" paper, perhaps revised once again, should help us engage in a multilateral conversation to find out, with due consideration given to all concerned, what is possible and what is not possible for any of us within the present denomination.

In the meantime, this book has attempted to lay out some of the meaning of Presbyterianism as seen from our perspective, some of the essentials of being Black and Presbyterian, and whether or not we remain within or decide to reconstitute ourselves outside the bounds of the Presbyterian Church (U.S.A.). Much of what we have discussed so far would be relevant to either decision.

Burdened But Not in Despair

As one peruses "Is This New Wine?" and a 1995 proposal of the African American Advisory Committee that suggests an African American nongeographic presbytery within the present denomination as a possible alternative to total withdrawal, an impression comes through loud and clear: Many younger clergy and laity feel overwhelmed by the glaring inconsistencies of the White church and the difficulty of being, at one and the same time, responsible to the African American community and loyal members of the Presbyterian Church. Any non-White person who has worked in this denomination at national and regional levels will sympathize with these younger members. There is a terrible frustration in being Black and Presbyterian. But it is no different from the frustration of being "born and bred Black" in America. Let's face it, we have a burden. We've always had a burden—one that is as old as our sojourn in this land and as exasperating as the condition Du Bois so aptly described as our "twoness ... two warring ideals in one dark body, whose dogged strength alone keeps it from being torn asunder."[5]

But we are not given to despair because we believe that it is not our "dogged strength alone" that keeps us whole, but the grace of God through Jesus Christ, the Burden-Bearer of the world.

In years past we were able to carry our burdens with a strange joy and sense of accomplishment. Our leaders surmounted many of the obstacles thrown before them by an ignorant and uncaring church. Moreover, by the salience of their arguments and the persuasiveness of their personalities, these leaders forced White folks to take Black folks seriously and, to some extent, absorb our mission into theirs without total coaptation. In the course of proceeding in this way, each of the two groups learned something valuable about the other, and the whole *missio Dei*, God's own mission to this planet, was advanced in the whole universe.

If Black theology has anything special to offer the "Is This New Wine?" discussion, it is to assert that whether or not our appropriation of God's mission is authentic, whether we are following Jesus or following some false messiah of our own ethnic invention—in other words, *the test of our apostolicity*—will be measured more by our deeds than by our creeds, our polities, or our politics. Black theology affirms that the deeds of Christians are the fruit of the grace of God through Christ; that they are performed in a routine struggle against those powers, religious and secular, that would rob us of our inheritance as the liberated children of God; and that we express our Blackness most perfectly and powerfully not when we act in splendid isolation, but when we bring from the treasure house of our African slave ancestors the gifts of struggle, suffering, and grace for the whole human family.

Thus a group of African American theologians, meeting at Virginia Union University in December 1984, promulgated an ecumenical statement ("Toward a Common Expression of Faith: A Black North American Perspective"), which declared

> It is in the Black Church's historic identification with marginality that Jesus is appropriated as the Black Messiah, the paradigm of our existential reality as an oppressed people and the affirmation of our survival and liberation. . . . [T]he search for an expression of [this] Apostolic faith must be multiracial and multicultural rather than captive to any one race, sex, class, or political ideology. . . . The faith once delivered to the apostles by Jesus Christ is for the whole world and must be capable of being transmitted and responded to by all.[6]

This does not automatically cancel out any justification for creating an African Presbyterian Church in America, but it does force us to ask some hard questions about the necessity and rightness of leaving the church under the presumption that in no other way can we pursue our historic vocation. Being a part of the Presbyterian Church (U.S.A.), as burdensome as it may be for even younger shoulders than ours, ought not put us in despair of fulfilling the destiny to which we have been called—a part of which is to help fulfill the prayer of our Lord in John 17:20–22: "I ask not only on behalf of these, but also on behalf of those who will believe in me through their word, that they may all be one. As you, Father, are in me and I am in you, may they also be in us, so that the world may believe that you have sent me. The glory that you have given me I have given them, so that they may be one, as we are one."

A Final Observation

We Black Presbyterians have a heritage—a heritage that we have been excavating from the quarries of history throughout this book; a heritage worth preserving and building on today.

But we also have a hope—a hope that is in Jesus Christ and what Christ has done for our salvation and the salvation of the world. This hope is partially expressed by our practical, daily commitment to the worldwide church that is Christ's body and to its peace and unity, that it might be purified and accomplish the mission for which Christ sent it into this world.

Today we see more clearly than we did in the 1960s that one part of that mission has to do with an Afrocentric orientation that critiques ways of looking at reality through the spectacles of White European and North American scholars who cast aspersion on any perception other than their own. It is a mission that lifts up our African and African American heritage as a spiritual legacy that, because it is a God-given expression of a common humanity, belongs not only to us but also to the whole world.

The hope we have is nothing less than the hope of our ancestors when they first heard the proclamation of the gospel in ancient Africa and then heard it again—filtered through the ethnocentric sieve of European civilization. It is a hope that, despite the chains, "the glory of the LORD [was being] revealed, and that all people [would] see it together" (Isa. 40:5). The hope was that freedom would one day conquer slavery; that justice would overcome injustice; that love would win out over every alienation and hatred; and that our children's children for generations to come would inherit a church in which people will be organically connected in ways that transcend all the barriers of gender, race, class, and culture.

It seems to some of us that not by giving up, but by demanding to be heard in the courts of the church and struggling to assume our rightful place in the development of an authentic Christian witness, we who are both Black and Presbyterian can make the day more speedily come when, as Col. 1:18–20 anticipates, Jesus Christ "might come to have first place in everything. For in him all the fullness of God was pleased to dwell, and through him God was pleased to reconcile to himself all things, whether on earth or in heaven, by making peace through the blood of his cross."

Perhaps the penultimate word should come from the younger voices in our churches. We were struck by the poignancy of an article in the May 1992 issue of *Perspectives*, written by an African American pastor who ruminated about his uncertainty on the night of his candidacy statement for ordination as a minister in the Presbyterian Church (U.S.A). His words, spoken for many of us who asked for ordination as ministers of Word and Sacrament in this church, echo the feeling of many who belong to the older generation of clergy:

> That night at First Presbyterian I realized that I would always have feelings of discontent in my chosen church. I mourn frequently because I do not have what I perceive as the cultural homogeneousness of the black church. On the night I became a candidate for ministry I did not understand that I would always mourn this loss. I am not alone in my grief; I hold it in common with the grief of my generation of African Americans who have attained middle-class status and are moving in realms unknown to our forebears and outside the confines of the traditional communal institutions that nurtured us.

> Yet, I am proud to be a Presbyterian. It has been my privilege to serve and to have access to structures that have allowed me to share the gospel in lands and with people who are more politically and socially marginalized than I ever can claim to have experienced in the United States. I am proud to be in a denomination that takes its theological heritage seriously and wrestles with it. And although I dislike being culturally marginal in the church, the irony of history is that the denomination needs the cultural and spiritual presence of my generation of African Americans to shed the denomination's negative elitist and racist past so as to reinvigorate the life of worship in the church as a whole. . . . As I think back to that night at First Presbyterian, I realize how much God was in that building calling me and my church to build up the body of Christ.[7]

But if the penultimate decision should come from the younger ordained clergy who must carry the burden of leadership in the years to come, the ultimate decision about "Is This New Wine?" must come from the people in the pews—the laity, both young and old. We who call ourselves the servants of God before the altar must give way to the servants of God before the hearth, the places of work, and the whirligig of worldly affairs. Not in the scholar's library nor in the sanctuary, but in these daily, dull, and ordinary places where the people of the pews ply their lives does God tear down and build up the ramparts of the secular as the chosen arena, the praxis-province of lay discipleship. There, where the people struggle for humanity and justice, is where the true servanthood of the church will herald if not usher in final consummation of the divine purpose. For this reason, we who are the ordained ministers of Word and Sacrament are nothing if we are not servants of the servants of God.

Accordingly, we end this book without a clear and final answer to the question "Is this new wine?" Is this proposal to leave the Presbyterian Church (U.S.A.) for a more perfect form of Christian community that will unite and strengthen various hemispheric strands of the African diaspora viable, feasible, and imperative for the future of African American Presbyterianism? The argument of the preceding pages has been cautiously against schism. Apart from the issue of viability and feasibility, we have raised the question of theological and practical necessity. We have asked if leaving the denomination at this time is really the only option available for the cultivation of a sound Afrocentric Presbyterianism. At the same time, we have commended the African American Advisory Committee and the younger clergy and laity who originated the "Is This New Wine?" document and are urgently recommending its adoption.

But the final decision must be made by the men and women who comprise the African American lay constituency on the eve and into the early years of the twenty-first century. We bring this discussion to a close, therefore, in the confidence that the Holy Spirit, who will lead us into all truth (John 16:12–15), will dwell in the midst of the sessions and congregations that must wrestle with these questions of Black identity and mission until they are convinced of the will of God for themselves. Some may decide, on the testimony of the Spirit, to stay. Some may decide, on the testimony of that same Spirit, to go. We can only surmise the rightness or wrongness of their choices. The Holy Spirit is the *pneuma*, the wind of God, "but you do not know where it comes from or where it goes" (John 3:8)—only that the Spirit moves variously among believers today no less than it moved within the fledgling church after the resurrection. We only know, as the old Negro spiritual tells us, that we have to go where the Spirit says go, and do what the Spirit says do.

In either case, if it is the Spirit of God, the Third Person of the Holy Trinity, who speaks, we can salvage the best of the past and be confident about the future. All we can say now is that we trust the Spirit to instruct the African American members of the Presbyterian Church (U.S.A.), if we are seriously open to being instructed, how to claim our ancient heritage and our future hope, either within or outside of this predominantly White denomination. As we study "Is This New Wine?" may that heavenly yet very earthbound voice be heard, and may we all, by the grace of the One who gives us the ability to hear what the Spirit says to the churches, be obedient to what we hear.

Questions for Discussion

Scripture for Reflection: James 4:1–10

1. How can African American male clergy demand to be fully accepted and respected by this denomination at large when they do not fully accept and respect African American clergywomen?

2. What do you consider to be the extreme crisis facing African American Presbyterians as we approach the twenty-first century?

3. What are your strongest reactions to the development of the African Presbyterian Church in America (APCA)? Would you make a commitment to supporting this denomination?

4. What is the Afrocentric movement? How might it impact the Presbyterian Church (U.S.A.)?

5. Does the fact that you are Black in a predominantly White denomination directly affect your ability to worship freely, respond to the needs of persons in your community, or participate in committees that are important to you?

6. Where do we go from here? What steps should now be taken to address the continuing dilemma of being Black and Presbyterian?

7. Does your congregation have plans to study the "Is This New Wine?" document?

Notes

Chapter 1

1. Albert J. Raboteau, *Slave Religion: The "Invisible Institution" in the Antebellum South* (New York: Oxford University Press, 1978), pp. 68–69.

Chapter 2

1. Charles C. Jones, *The Religious Instruction of the Negroes in the United States* (Savannah: T. Purse Co., 1842; reprint, New York: Books for Libraries Press, 1971), p. 127.

2. *David Walker's Appeal: To the Coloured Citizens of the World, but in particular, and very expressly, to those of the United States of America,* first published in October 1829 by David Walker (Baltimore: Black Classic Press, 1993).

3. Richard Wright, Jr., *The Centennial Encyclopedia of the Methodist Episcopal Church, 1816–1916* (Philadelphia: AME Church, 1916), p. 11.

4. W. E. Burghardt Du Bois, *The Souls of Black Folk* (New York: Washington Square Press, 1970), pp. 163, 165.

5. Vincent Harding, "The Religion of Black Power," in *The Religious Situation: 1968;* edited by Donald R. Cutler (Boston: Beacon Press, 1968).

Chapter 3

1. John T. McNeill, *The History and Character of Calvinism* (New York: Oxford University Press), p. 178. [Note: This phrase is found in a letter Knox sent to an English friend, Mrs. Anne Locke, in December 1556.]

2. Darius L. Swann, *All-Black Governing Bodies: The History and Contributions of All-Black Governing Bodies in the Predecessor Denominations of the Presbyterian Church (U.S.A.)* (Louisville, Kentucky: The Office of the General Assembly, PC(USA), 1996), p. 16.

3. W. H. Franklin, *The Early History of the Presbyterian Church in the U.S.A. Among the Negroes* (Philadelphia: Presbyterian Historical Society, n.d.).

4. Cited in Andrew E. Murray, *Presbyterians and the Negro—A History* (Philadelphia: Presbyterian Historical Society, 1966), p. 10.

5. Cited in Ernest Trice Thompson, *Presbyterians in the South.* 3 vols. (Atlanta: John Knox Press, 1963–1973).

6. Samuel Cornish, *The Colored American*, March 11, 1837.

7. Murray, *Presbyterians and the Negro*, p. 19.

8. George Bourne, *Picture of Slavery in the United States of America* (Middletown, Conn.: Hunt, 1934), p. 188.

9. Swann, *All-Black Governing Bodies*, p. 17.

10. A. B. Hyde, *The Story of Methodism* (Greenfield, Mass.: Willey & Co., 1887), p. 63.

Chapter 4

1. Matthew Anderson in a letter to Francis J. Grimke, dated May 29, 1916, as cited in Carter G. Woodson, *Works of Francis J. Grimke*, vol. 4 (Washington, D. C.: Associated Publications, 1990), p. 166.

2. Cited in Darius L. Swann, *All-Black Governing Bodies: The History and Contributions of All-Black Governing Bodies in the Predecessor Denominations of the Presbyterian Church (U.S.A.)* (Louisville, Kentucky: The Office of the General Assembly, PC(USA), 1996), p. 103.

3. Andrew E. Murray, *Presbyterians and the Negro—A History* (Philadelphia: Presbyterian Historical Society, 1966), p. 198.

Chapter 6

1. W. E. Burghardt Du Bois, *The Souls of Black Folk* (New York: Washington Square Press, 1970), p. 3.

Chapter 7

1. From the preface to an official NBPC document dated December 31, 1994.

2. "A Message to the Churches from Oakland, California," Statement by the National Committee of Black Churchmen, Third Annual Convocation, Nov. 11–14, 1969, as cited in Gayraud S. Wilmore and James H. Cone, eds., *Black Theology: A Documentary History, 1966–1992* (Maryknoll, New York: Orbis Books, 1979), p. 104.

Chapter 9

1. The term *Afrocentric,* according to its most prominent interpreter, Professor Molefi Kete Asante of Temple University, means viewing reality with African rather than European or Euro-American spectacles. It presents a radical critique of so-called universal truth as defined by White scholars by "taking the globe and turning it over so that we see all the possibilities of a world where Africa ... is subject and not object" (Molefi Kete Asante, *The Afrocentric Idea* [Philadelphia: Temple University Press, 1987], p. 3).

Chapter 10

1. "Is This New Wine?" Presbyterians for Prayer, Study, and Action Office of Racial and Cultural Diversity, Racial Ethnic Ministry Unit PC(USA) cover letter, p. ii.

2. Ibid., p. 20.

3. Molefi Kete Asante, *The Afrocentric Idea* (Philadelphia: Temple University Press, 1987), pp. 5–6.

4. "Is This New Wine?" pp. 10–11; italics added.

5. W. E. Burghardt Du Bois, *The Souls of Black Folk* (New York: Washington Square Press, 1970), p. 3.

6. David T. Shannon and Gayraud S. Wilmore, eds., *Black Witness to the Apostolic Faith* (Grand Rapids: Wm. B. Eerdmans Publishing Co., 1985), p. 69.

7. Randal M. Jelks, "Waters of Babylon: To Be an African American Presbyterian," *Perspectives* (May 1992): 9.

Resources for Further Study

The following list of resources is by no means exhaustive. It does not include many helpful works still in print, many different kinds of educational helps—maps, posters, multimedia kits, tracts, rituals, games, and so forth—that have been developed in recent years to help individuals and congregations study the Bible, Black history, and Black culture. Nor does it include many resources on Black women's struggle against sexism, multicultural resources now available to inform ethnic groups in the church about their counterparts from other national and cultural backgrounds, and conference statements and pronouncements written to bring people of various races and ethnic identities together for mutual support and collaboration.

Except for the books, many of these materials may be ordered from the Presbyterian Distribution Service (PDS), located at the denominational headquarters: 100 Witherspoon Street, Louisville, KY 40202-1396. It is helpful to telephone first at (800) 524-2612.

The reader should consult *The PC(USA) Guide to Resources,* compiled by Dr. Arlene W. Gordon, Associate for Resource Center Development and Educational Ministry Advocates Support of the Presbyterian Church (U.S.A.). The project team, convened by Dr. Gordon for the purpose of preparing and publishing this guide, includes several members of the church's national staff in Louisville, Kentucky. Michael Purintun, Senior Administrative Assistant, was the project recorder. This invaluable and comprehensive resource guide can be ordered from the Presbyterian Distribution Service, Presbytel (800-872-3283), or as a last resort, from the Office of Resource Center Development (800-411-7950).

Audiovisuals

Alex Haley: The Search for Roots. Color film, 18 mins. Rent from Films for the Humanities, P.O. Box 2053, Princeton, NJ 08540.

Between a Rock and a Hard Place. Video and study guide on racism. Rent from Racial Ethnic Ministries, PC(USA).

Black Religion I and II. Color filmstrips of 80–90 frames each. Scholastic Audiovisual Center, 904 Sylvan Ave., Englewood Cliffs, NJ 07632.

Celebrating Our Differences, Sharing Our Gifts. Video. Rent from Racial Ethnic Ministries, PC(USA).

The Ebony Chalice: Racism and the Church. Video and study guide on racism and Black Presbyterianism. Buy or rent from the Synod of the Trinity, PC(USA).

Eyes on the Prize. Video. A PBS special on the Civil Rights movement. Rent from Racial Ethnic Ministries, PC(USA).

The Journey Continues: African Christians Speak. Video and book on sustainable development, reconciliation, African theologies, and evangelism. Buy or rent from PDS, PC(USA).

Let the Church Say Amen! Cokesbury Service Center, 201 Eighth Ave., South, Nashville, TN 37202.

Lift Every Voice—The Bible in an Age of Diversity. Cain Hope Felder and Tony Campolo. Video for a five-part Bible study on understanding our diversity from a biblical perspective. Rent from Racial Ethnic Ministries, PC(USA).

New Roads to Faith: Black Perspectives in Church Education. Filmstrip developed by Yvonne V. Delk. 317 color frames, guide, script, and audiocassettes. Curriculum Services, PC(USA).

Racial Ethnic Convocation: 1993. Video on the proceedings of the interethnic gathering of Presbyterians. Rent from Racial Ethnic Ministries, PC(USA).

Two Black Churches. Color film, 20 min. Center for Southern Folklore, 1216 Peabody Ave., P.O. Box 4081, Memphis, TN 38104.

Booklets, Packets, and Curriculum Series

Africa: Country Profiles. Packet of information about African churches in 20 countries. Mission Interpretation, PC(USA).

Africa Reading and Viewing List. Brochure expressing solidarity with Africans through church partners. Mission Interpretation, PC(USA).

Africa Slide Set. Set of 20 slides illustrating life in Africa and Presbyterian churches in mission there. PDS #225-93-718.

Afrocentric Spirituality and Ministry. Video in two sets distributed by the Black Congregational Enhancement Unit of the PC(USA).

America's Original Sin: A Study Guide on White Racism. Nine study sessions with questions for reflection and action. National Ministries Division (NMD), PC(USA).

Anti-Bias Curriculum: Tools for Empowering Young People. Fostering children's healthy identity and attitudes toward race, ethnicity, gender, and disabilities. NMD, PC(USA).

Black Presbyterians in Mission. Occasional publication of the PC(USA). Basic information on church-based community organizing. NMD, PC(USA).

Criminal Justice Sunday Program Guide. Resources for worship, reflection, and action. Includes *Justice and Only Justice. . . . People of Color and the Criminal Justice System.* PDS #72-630-95-711.

Decoding Diversity and Inclusiveness in the Presbyterian Church (U.S.A.). PDS #258-91-605.

Design for Evangelism in the Black Presbyterian Church, by William G. Gillespie. Jointly published by UPC(USA), Second Cumberland Presbyterian Church, and the PC(USA). Order from PDS.

Dynamics of Church Growth, by Lonnie J. Oliver. A resource for Black Presbyterian renewal and growth. Order from PDS.

The Effective Black Church: Growing Your Church for the Twenty-first Century. Booklet by Bennie E. Goodwin. Order from Goodpatrick Publishers, 45 North 21st Street, East Orange, NJ 07017.

Great Kings of Africa. Portfolio of fourteen color reprints of paintings with captions on the African heritage. Order from Anheuser-Busch, Inc., 2800 S. Ninth St., St. Louis, MO 63118.

Identity Crisis: Blacks in Predominantly White Denominations. Booklet by Gayraud S. Wilmore. Order from the Black Council of the Reformed Church in America.

Intercultural Interactions: A Practical Guide. Study guide for training in how to relate across cultures. NMD, PC(USA).

Is This New Wine? Policy paper with study guide on Black Presbyterian renewal by the African American Advisory Committee. Order from Racial Ethnic Ministries, PC(USA).

Lift Every Voice and Sing: A Collection of Afro-American Spirituals and Other Songs. Contains 151 pieces of music from the African American religious heritage. Order from the Church Hymnal Corporation, 800 Second Ave., New York, NY 10017.

Periscope I, II, and III. Booklets of essays on Black Presbyterian history and mission published by the National Black Presbyterian Caucus and its predecessor organization. Inquire for copies at the NMD, PC(USA).

Soulful Worship. A 160-page booklet by Clarence J. Rivers dealing with Black Christian worship. An aid to creative worship. Order from the National Office of Black Catholics, 1234 Massachusetts Ave., N.W., Washington, DC 20005.

Women of Color Partnership. Brochure promoting responsible decision making in the reproductive choice movement. NMD, PC(USA).

Books

Asante, Molefi Kete. *The Afrocentric Idea*. Philadelphia: Temple University Press, 1987.

———. *Kemet, Afrocentricity, and Knowledge*. Trenton, NJ: Africa World Press, 1990.

Bailey, Randall, and Jacqueline Grant, eds. *The Recovery of Black Presence: An Interdisciplinary Exploration*. Nashville: Abingdon Press, 1995.

Barber, Jesse Belmont. *Climbing Jacob's Ladder: Story of the Presbyterian Church (U.S.A.) among the Negroes*. Published for the Board of National Ministries, Presbyterian Church (U.S.A.) New York: Presbyterian Distribution Service, 1952.

———. A *History of the Presbyterian Church Among Negroes in the U.S.A.* PC(USA), 1936.

Batchelor, Alex R. *Jacob's Ladder: Negro Work of the Presbyterian Church in the United States*. Richmond: PCUS, 1953.

Ben-Jochannan, Yosef. *African Origins of the Major "Western Religions."* Chesterfield, VA: Alkebu-Lan Books, 1970.

Boesak, Allan. *Black and Reformed: Apartheid, Liberation, and the Calvinist Tradition*. Maryknoll, NY: Orbis Books, 1984.

Cannon, Katie G. *Black Womanist Ethics*. Decatur, GA: Scholars Press, 1988.

Carter, Harold A. *The Prayer Tradition of Black People*. Valley Forge, PA: Judson Press, 1976.

Cone, James H. *Black Theology and Black Power*. New York: Seabury Press, 1969.

———. *A Black Theology of Liberation: Twentieth Anniversary with Critical Responses*. Maryknoll, NY: Orbis Books, 1990.

Cone, James H., and Gayraud S. Wilmore, eds. *Black Theology: A Documentary History, 1966—1992*. 2 vols. Maryknoll, NY: Orbis Books, 1992.

———. *For My People: Black Theology and the Black Church*. Maryknoll, NY: Orbis Books, 1984.

Copher, Charles B. *Black Biblical Studies*. Chicago: Black Light Fellowship, 1993.

Costen, Melva W. *African American Christian Worship*. Nashville: Abingdon Press, 1993.

Creel, Margaret W. *"A Peculiar People": Slave Religion and Community Culture among the Gullahs.* New York: New York University Press, 1988.

Diop, Cheikh Anta. *The African Origin of Civilization: Myth or Reality?* Translated by Mercer Cook. New York: Lawrence Hill & Co., 1974.

Dixon, Rita, and Michael Dash, Darius Swann, and Ndugu T'Ofori-Atta, eds. *African Roots: Toward an Afrocentric Christian Witness.* Lithonia, GA: SCP: Third World Literature Publishing House, 1994.

Douglas, Kelly Brown. *The Black Christ.* Maryknoll, NY: Orbis Books, 1994.

Drake, St. Clair. *The Redemption of Africa and Black Religion.* Chicago: Third World Press, 1970.

Du Bois, W. E. Burghardt. *The Gift of Black Folk.* New York: Washington Square Press, 1970.

———. *The Souls of Black Folk.* New York: Washington Square Press, 1970.

———. *The World and Africa.* New York: International Publications, Co. 1978.

Eugene, Toinette. *Lifting As We Climb: A Womanist Ethic of Care.* Nashville: Abingdon Press, 1996.

Evans, James H., Jr. *We Have Been Believers: An African American Systematic Theology.* Minneapolis: Fortress Press, 1992.

Felder, Cain Hope, ed. *Stony the Road We Trod: African American Biblical Interpretation.* Minneapolis: Fortress Press, 1991.

———. *Troubling Biblical Waters: Race, Class, and Family.* Maryknoll, NY: Orbis Books, 1989.

Franklin, Robert M. *Liberating Visions: Human Fulfillment and Social Justice in African American Thought.* Minneapolis: Fortress Press, 1990.

George, Carol V. R. *Segregated Sabbaths: Richard Allen and the Emergence of Independent Black Churches, 1760–1840.* New York: Oxford University Press, 1973.

Grant, Jacquelyn. *White Women's Christ and Black Women's Jesus: Feminist Christology and Womanist Response.* Decatur, GA: Scholars Press, 1989.

Harding, Vincent. *Hope and History: Why We Must Share the Story of the Movement.* Maryknoll, NY: Orbis Books, 1990.

———. *There Is a River: The Black Struggle for Freedom in America.* New York: Harcourt Brace Jovanovich, 1981.

Harris, Forrest E. *Ministry for Social Crisis: Theology and Praxis in the Black Church Tradition.* Macon, GA: Mercer University Press, 1993.

Harris, Forrest E., ed. *What Does It Mean to Be Black and Christian? Pulpit, Pew, and Academy in Dialogue.* Marlton, NJ: Townsend Press, 1995.

Harris, James H. *Pastoral Theology: A Black-Church Perspective.* Minneapolis: Fortress Press, 1991.

Hayes, Diana L. *And Still We Rise: An Introduction to Black Liberation Theology.* Mahwah, NJ: Paulist Press, 1996.

————. *Hagar's Daughters: Womanist Ways of Being in the World.* Mahwah, NJ: Paulist Press, 1995.

Holloway, James E., ed. *Africanisms in American Culture.* Bloomington, IN: Indiana University Press, 1990.

Hood, Robert E. *Must God Remain Greek? Afro Cultures and God-Talk.* Minneapolis: Fortress Press, 1990.

Hopkins, Dwight N., and George Cummings. *Cut Loose Your Stammering Tongue: Black Theology and the Slave Narratives.* Maryknoll, NY: Orbis Books, 1991.

————. *Shoes That Fit Our Feet: Sources for a Constructive Black Theology.* Maryknoll, NY: Orbis Books, 1993.

Jackson, John G. *Introduction to African Civilizations.* New York: Citadel Press, 1970.

Jahn, Janheinz. *Muntu: An Outline of the New African Culture.* New York: Grove Press, 1961.

Jones, William. *God in the Ghetto.* Elgin, IL: Progressive Baptist Publishing House, 1979.

King, Martin L., Jr. *Strength to Love.* Cleveland, OH: Collins-World Publishing Co., 1963.

————. *Where Do We Go from Here: Chaos or Community?* New York: Harper & Row, 1967.

King, Noel Q. *Christian and Muslim in Africa.* New York: Harper & Row, 1971.

Levine, Lawrence. *Black Culture and Black Consciousness.* New York: Oxford University Press, 1977.

Lewis, Nantawan Boonprasat, and others, eds. *Sisters Struggling in the Spirit: Women of Color Theological Anthology.* Louisville: PC(USA), 1994.

Lincoln, C. Eric, and Lawrence H. Mamiya. *The Black Church in the African American Experience*. Durham, NC: Duke University Press, 1990.

_____. *Race, Religion, and the Continuing American Dilemma*. New York: Hill & Wang, 1984.

Lovell, John. *Black Song: The Forge and the Flame, The Story of How the Afro-American Spiritual Was Hammered Out*. New York: Macmillan, 1972.

Marable, Manning. *Blackwater: Historical Studies in Race, Class Consciousness, and Revolution*. Black Praxis Press, 1981.

Mays, Benjamin E. *The Negro's God: As Reflected in His Literature*. New York: Atheneum, 1969.

Mbiti, John S. *African Religions and Philosophy*. Westport, CT: Praeger Publications, 1970.

McCall, Emmanuel L., ed. *Black Church Lifestyles*. Nashville: Broadman Press, 1986.

McClain, William B. *Travelling Light: Pluralism and Pilgrimage*. New York: Friendship Press, 1981.

McCray, Walter A. *The Black Presence in the Bible*. Chicago: Black Light Fellowship, 1989.

Mitchell, Henry. *Black Belief: Folk Beliefs of Blacks in America and West Africa*. New York: Harper & Row, 1975.

_____. *Soul Theology: The Heart of American Black Culture*. Nashville: Abingdon Press, 1991.

Murray, Andrew E. *Presbyterians and the Negro—A History*. Philadelphia: Presbyterian Historical Society, 1966.

Opoku, Kofi Asare. *West African Traditional Religion*. FEP International Private Ltd., 1978.

Parker, Inez Moore. *The Rise and Decline of the Program of Education for Black Presbyterians of the United Presbyterian Church U.S.A. (1865–1970)*. San Antonio: Trinity University Press, 1977.

Raboteau, Albert J. *Slave Religion: The "Invisible Institution" in the Antebellum South*. New York: Oxford University Press, 1978.

Riggs, Marcia. *Awake, Arise, and Act: A Womanist Call for Black Liberation*. New York: Pilgrim Press, 1995.

Roberts, J. Deotis. *Liberation and Reconciliation: A Black Theology.* Maryknoll, NY: Orbis Books, 1994.

———. *The Prophethood of Black Believers: An African American Political Theology for Ministry.* Maryknoll, NY: Orbis Books, 1995.

Sanders, Cheryl J., ed. *Living the Intersection: Womanism and Afrocentrism in Theology.* Minneapolis: Fortress Press, 1994.

Sanneh, Lamin. *West African Christianity: The Religious Impact.* Maryknoll, NY: Orbis Books, 1983.

Sawyer, Mary. *Black Ecumenism: Implementing the Demands of Justice.* Philadelphia: Trinity Press International, 1994.

Sernett, Milton C., ed. *Afro-American Religious History: A Documentary Witness.* Durham, NC: Duke University Press, 1985.

Shannon, David T., and Gayraud S. Wilmore, eds. *Black Witness to the Apostolic Faith.* Grand Rapids: Wm. B. Eerdmans Publishing Co., 1985.

Sobel, Michal. *Travelin' On: The Slave Journey to an Afro-Baptist Faith.* Westport, CT: Greenwood Press, 1979.

Stewart, Carlyle F., III. *African American Church Growth: Twelve Principles for Prophetic Ministry.* Nashville: Abingdon Press, 1994.

———. *Soul Survivors: An African American Spirituality.* Louisville: Westminster John Knox Press, 1997.

Stroupe, Gibson, and Inez Fleming. *While We Run This Race: Confronting the Power of Racism in a Southern Church.* Maryknoll, NY: Orbis Books, 1995.

Swann, Darius L. *All-Black Governing Bodies: The History and Contributions of All-Black Governing Bodies in the Predecessor Denominations of the Presbyterian Church (U.S.A.).* Louisville: The Office of the General Assembly, PC(USA), 1996.

Swift, David E. *Black Prophets of Justice: Activist Clergy Before the Civil War.* Baton Rouge, LA: Louisiana State University Press, 1989.

Thomas, Latta R. *Biblical Faith and the Black American.* Valley Forge, PA: Judson Press, 1976.

Thurman, Howard. *Deep River: Reflections on the Religious Insight of Certain of the Negro Spirituals.* New York: Harper & Brothers, 1955.

———. *Jesus and the Disinherited.* Nashville: Abingdon-Cokesbury Press, 1949.

T'Ofori-Atta, Ndugu. *Christkwanza: An African American Church Liturgy.* Clinton, NY: Strugglers' Community Press, 1991.

Townes, Emilie. *In a Blaze of Glory: Womanist Spirituality as Social Witness.* Nashville: Abingdon Press, 1995.

Van Sertima, Ivan, ed. "Nile Valley Civilizations: Proceedings of the Nile Valley Conference," *Journal of African Civilizations,* 1985.

Walker, Wyatt Tee. *Somebody's Calling My Name: Black Sacred Music and Social Change.* Valley Forge, PA: Judson Press, 1979.

Walsh, Martin De Porres. *The Ancient Black Christians.* Julian Richardson Associates, 1969.

Washington, James M. *Conversations with God: Two Centuries of Prayers by African Americans.* New York: HarperCollins, 1994.

Weems, Renita. *Just a Sister Away: A Womanist Vision of Women's Relationships in the Bible.* San Diego, CA: LuraMedia, 1988.

Weisbord, Robert G. *Ebony Kinship: Africa, Africans, and the Afro-Americans.* Westport, CT: Greenwood Press, 1973.

West, Cornel. *Prophesy Deliverance! An Afro-American Revolutionary Christianity.* Philadelphia: Westminster Press, 1982.

———. *Race Matters.* Boston: Beacon Press, 1993.

Williams, Delores. *Sisters in the Wilderness.* Maryknoll, NY: Orbis Books, 1993.

Wilmore, Gayraud S., *Black Religion and Black Radicalism.* 3rd ed. Maryknoll, NY: Orbis Books, 1988.

———. *Last Things First: Eschatology in Black.* Philadelphia: Westminster Press, 1982.

———., ed. *African American Religious Studies: An Interdisciplinary Anthology.* Durham, NC: Duke University Press, 1989.

Wilson, Frank T. *Black Presbyterians in Ministry.* New York: Vocation Agency, UPC(USA), 1980.

Wimberly, Anne S. *Soul Stories: African American Christian Education.* Nashville: Abingdon Press, 1994.

Wimberly, Edward P., and Anne Streaty. *Liberation and Human Wholeness: The Conversion Experiences of Black People in Slavery and Freedom.* Nashville: Abingdon Press, 1986.

Woodson, Carter G. *The History of the Negro Church.* Washington, DC: Associated Publications, 1972.

———. *The Mis-Education of the Negro.* Nashville: Winston-Derek Pubs., Inc., 1990.

Young, Josiah U. *Black and African Theologies: Siblings or Distant Cousins?* Maryknoll, NY: Orbis Books, 1986.

Reference Works and Journals

Directory of African American Religious Bodies: A Compendium by the Howard University School of Divinity, edited by Wardell J. Payne. Washington, DC: Howard University Press, 1991.

Encyclopedia of African-American Culture and History, edited by Jack Salzman, David L. Smith, and Cornel West. Five volumes. New York: Simon & Schuster, 1996.

Encyclopedia of African American Religions, edited by Larry G. Murphy, J. Gordon Melton, and Gary L. Ward. New York: Garland Publishing Co., 1993.

The Journal of the Interdenominational Theological Center. Published quarterly by the ITC, 700 Martin Luther King Jr. Drive, Atlanta, GA 30314.

The Journal of Religious Thought. Published quarterly by the Howard University School of Divinity, 1240 Randolph Street, N.E., Washington, DC 20017.

A Pictorial History of Black Americans, edited by Langston Hughes, Milton Meltzer, and C. Eric Lincoln. Fourth Revised Edition, New York: Crown Publishers, 1973.

Reader's Notes

Reader's Notes